CONSISTENT CUSTOMERS

By Jon Riley

www.YourBusinessWithin.com

"There is no traffic on that extra mile"

1. Select
2. Serve
3. Succeed

**Tips, Techniques and
Strategies for Growing
ANY Type of Business**

Dedicated to:
Joel Bauer & Martin Howey
Co-Authors

To my awesome dad:
Orbin K Riley
who defined Tenacity

And to my Small Business
Mentor **Ronald L Smith**

Before we begin, I would like to introduce myself. I am a husband, a father of two & a small business owner. Having my own small business for 30 years has enabled me to take care of my family, **live life by design and not by default**, pay for my own health insurance & fund my retirement. I developed a small business system called **"Your Business Within"**. It is a three-step process that will potentially empower anyone to save themselves a thirty-year learning curve in starting their own small business. Step One is to **SELECT** your business name and type to get started. You will design your business cards, flyers, and build your Free Website. You will have your phone, phone number and maybe some starter testimonials. Step One is 10 easy to follow modules for **any type** of business to get started with little to no money in 30 days or less.

It's simple, it's easy and it works.

Step Two is to **SERVE.** This is where you learn "how to" run a small service business. Plumbing, heating, electrical, dog walking, maid or cleaning service, massage therapy, plant watering, hair stylist, computer repair, fitness trainer, martial arts instructor, window washer or even a Handyman service. **Any Service can be turned into a Business.** Start yours ASAP!

Step Three is to **SUCCEED.** You now have a real business and are ready to grow & apply to my 90 day or one-year Business Mentorship.

Bonus #1 in my system is "How to Manage an Apartment Building". Live Rent Free & use that money to fund your Roth I.R.A **Bonus #2** is how to invest that money Tax Free. I created a six-figure retirement for myself and my wife by purchasing empty lots through Online Auctions and selling them to the neighbors. I did this inside my Roth IRA creating tax free profits.

Napoleon Hill took information from successful people, repurposed it and put it into a book that became one of the most successful books of all time. **"Think and Grow Rich".** Thank you, Joel and Martin, for your knowledge and gifting me a license to this book. I have updated a lot of things and I teach micro trainings at the end of each of the 7 chapters. My autobiography is called:

"Y-Not-You" I share with you how I went from a Hillbilly Hundredaire to a Blue Collar Thousandaire. **www.JonRileyIRA.com**
Now enjoy:

"Consistent Customers"

Table of Contents

Introduction

If someone could wave a magic wand and suddenly change something about your chosen profession or business, what one thing would you have them change?

Would you have them provide you with an easier way to contact more, better-qualified prospects? And would you want those prospects as well as your current customers to view you as even more of a professional, or maybe even an "expert" in your field?

You may be good now, but how would you like to be even better at making more effective, more persuasive presentations? Perhaps you would like to be more effective at closing sales or handling objections. Or, is repeat business more important to you?

What if your current customers felt that you were the only person or the only business who understood and could effectively serve their specialized, unique and individual needs?

Or, how about referrals? Take the best customer you have right now. How would you like to have more contacts just like them than you could possibly handle? What one thing would you change to make you a better, happier, and more productive businessperson?

In the chapters to follow, we'll be discussing not only these areas, but other factors that are critical for you to realize real business success. Throughout the pages of this manual we'll explore some of the most effective ideas and field-proven methods and techniques that you can begin to put to use immediately to help you increase your sales, improve your business, overcome some of your most difficult problems and challenges, gain extra income, have more free time, and find a renewed enjoyment from your chosen business.

Increasing Your Effectiveness

You and I both know that it's no secret that things are changing today, faster than ever before. Technology has become more sophisticated, competition more keen, and consumers – the people who buy your products and services – have become more educated and aware.

And with the wide variety of choices your customers or clients have, not only in similar products and services from different companies, but also in the individual people they deal with, it stands to reason that the more skillful and professional you are at meeting your customer's needs, the bigger advantage you can command, and the more effective and successful you can become.

If you're really going to be effective and successful in the marketplace today, it is necessary, even vital, that you continually change, improve, adjust and up-date your selling, service, and problem-solving skills, as well as your methods of marketing and general business operation. It has been said, (and you've no doubt heard) that:

> **"People don't care how much you know,
> until they know how much you care."**

One of the best and most effective ways you can show your prospects and customers you care is by helping them solve their problems in a satisfactory, cost-effective, and professional manner.

Exposure to New Ideas

And that's what this program is all about. It has been written with the goal of helping you become the best you can be at what you do professionally.

Naturally, this program doesn't claim, nor does it pretend, to have all the answers to all your business problems. No book, course or seminar could do that.

Rather, the objective of this program is to expose you to some tried, tested, and field-proven ideas, concepts, and techniques that have worked for other business people much like you.

Once acquainted with new information and ideas, it will then be up to you to decide which ideas can best be tailored to your own individual business situation, and how you will begin to use them to better serve your customers and prospects.

The goal of this program is not to try to make you a marketing expert, but rather, to provide you with some of the tools the experts and those who are already successful in business are currently using.

Together, we'll explore specific marketing, sales, customer service, and business building techniques that others have used to significantly increase their businesses and incomes with very little extra effort.

You will most likely find that many of these ideas will be easy to implement, and you'll be able to begin using them right away. Others may take a little longer to gear up for. And still others may not be right for you or your operation at all. That's okay. It's not possible to provide 100% usable ideas for every person in every situation.

But if you get just one or two good, usable ideas that you can put into your business operation that makes a difference, then your time, effort and money will be well invested.

How We Retain Information

Getting a new idea is one thing, but what you do with it once you have it, is just as important as getting it in the first place. Studies on retention show that you remember:

- 10% of what you read,
- 22% of what you hear,
- 37% of what you see,
- 56% of what you see and hear, and up to
- 86% of what you see, hear and do.

So, an idea that is heard but not acted on is only half as likely to be retained as an idea that is actually put into practice. With that concept in mind then, it is important to understand that if the information presented in this book is to be of any real value to you, it must not only be read, it must be applied. That is to say, it must be experienced, or acted on. And that means it's going to take some effort on your part.

In their book, *The Knowing-Doing Gap,* authors, Jeffrey Pheffer and Robert L. Sutton mention that every year there are 1,700 new business books published, $60 billion spent on training, $43 billion spent on consultants and our universities turn out 80,000 graduates with MBA's. Yet, most businesses continue to operate day in and day out in much the same ways as they've always done.

You see, knowledge without action is no better than no knowledge at all. Just knowing isn't enough. You've got to do something with what you to know.

The ideas presented in this manual work. They're not theory. They're not speculation on what "should" work. And they're not philosophical musings. These ideas, concepts and techniques are currently in use by business owners across the country in one form or another. They're being proven in actual field use day in and day out.

They work for others, and they can work for you. But you're going to have to take the time to study them, understand them and make the necessary modifications to tailor them to your own personal and business style and operation. And then finally, you're going to have to apply them in your business.

Five Steps of Learning and Retention

Learning – the acquisition of new information or knowledge, and Retention – the ability to capture that information and recall it when wanted or needed, is actually a process that involves five steps:

First, is **Impact.** That is, actually receiving the idea in your mind. Impact can be in the form of a word, a visual observation or a concept. It makes no difference. Your mind isn't capable of making a distinction between a visual or an actual experience. Nor is it capable of determining the difference between a conscious or an unconscious impact an idea may have on you. As far as your mind is concerned, those experiences are all the same and your mind will accept them, regardless.

If information or an experience appears real to your mind, your emotions and nervous system will react as though it were actually real.

To illustrate this point, try this simple experiment:

Seat yourself in a comfortable chair, feet flat on the floor and your hands resting comfortably in your lap.

Close your eyes, take a deep breath, let it out slowly and relax. Take another one. Let it out slowly. Relax even more.

Picture in your mind a lemon resting on a table in front of you. Visualize it. See it clearly. Look at its shape – its color – its texture.

Now, mentally reach out with your hand and pick up the lemon. Bring it up to your face. Look at it closely. Squeeze it. Do you notice how firm it feels? Feel the texture of the lemon's dimply and waxy skin. Notice the lemon's yellow color and round shape, with its pointy ends.

Now, hold it up to your nose. Smell it. Do you notice the lemon's citrusy smell?

Place the lemon on the table and mentally pick up a knife that's laying nearby. Cut the lemon in two.

Pick up one half of the lemon and see the juice dripping from it. Bring the lemon up to your nose. Smell it again. Now bite into the lemon.

What's happening to you right now? Is saliva flooding your mouth, both in your mind, as well as physically?

Now consider what just happened. In actuality, there was no lemon. You just pictured one in your mind. While this was just a mental exercise, and the lemon was just imagined, chances are, if you are like most people, the mental image you were playing on the screen of your mind triggered certain responses which manifested themselves physically. So, you can see by this demonstration, that *Impact*, is a critical step involved in the process of learning and retention.

The second step is **Repetition.** One university study revealed that an idea that was read or heard only one time was 66% forgotten within 24 hours. But if that same idea was read or heard repeatedly for 8 days, up to 90% of it could be retained at the end of the eight days.

So, once you've read this manual all the way through, go back and read it again. But this time read with a highlighter, a pencil and notepad handy. Mark up the book. Write down the ideas you feel fit your personal business situation. This repetition will help you retain more of the information than if you had read it only once.

The third step in the learning and retention process is **Utilization.**

This is the "doing" step. It is here that neuromuscular pathways are actually developed, creating a "mind-muscle memory." And according to the study quoted earlier, once you physically experience an action, it becomes twice as easy to recall as if you had heard it only.

Fourth, is **Internalization?** Actually, making the idea a part of you. That may involve some customizing or tailoring of the idea to fit your situation or style, but it is vitally important for you to personalize the idea and make it "yours."

The fifth step is **Reinforcement.** In order to maximize the effectiveness of an idea, you should continually be looking for ways to support and strengthen it. The more you can support the idea, the more you will believe it, the longer you will retain it, and the more effective it will become in helping you serve your customers' needs.

Now, what does all this have to do with your business? Simply, this. In your daily business and personal activities, as well as throughout your experience with the information presented in this book, you are going to be exposed to a great number of ideas.

Some will be brand new, that is, you've never heard them before. Some will be ideas you have heard in the past, but have forgotten. And others will be ideas you come up with on your own as a result of something that was triggered in your mind as you read. Understanding and applying these five steps in the learning and retention process can help you retain more of what you read and experience.

Action Makes the Difference

It's important to keep an open mind as you read, hear, or otherwise experience ideas that can help you. Try not to judge them or cast them aside too quickly because they don't sound good, they're not part of your personality or make-up, or because you may have heard them before.

Instead, consider these courses of actions:

If you've heard an idea before, say to yourself, "Yes, I've heard that before, but am I using it?" If not, "Why not?"

If you are currently using the idea, ask yourself, "How effective am I at using it? How can I 'plus', or improve on it to make it even more effective for me and my business?"

Next, ask yourself this question: "What will I do as a result of what I've learned?"

Remember, it's not *what* you know — it's what you *do* that counts. Ideas are powerful. And good ideas are really important for any business. They're what keeps your interest up and your business fresh and alive and growing. And put into action, good ideas can make a huge difference in the way you do business, the results you realize, the fun you have, and the profits you make. This manual is full of good, practical, and usable ideas that can help make that big difference for you. But it's up to you to tailor them to your own unique situation, and more importantly, to put them into action.

The Business You're In

If you don't learn another thing from our time together, remember this...

You're NOT in the (What business you're in) business...
You're in the *MARKETING* business.

Read those sentences again... and again... and again. Digest them. Understand them. Internalize them. Make them an integral part of your business philosophy. Because unless and until you do, your business will be no better and no different than any of the other choices your prospects and customers can select to do business with.

Let me explain by using the insurance profession as an example, and as I do, think about how these principles might apply to your business.

It's a well-known fact that very few people (if any at all), want to actually buy an insurance policy. It's true, they may want the benefits, security and piece of mind that insurance provides them and their families or their business, but they don't necessarily want to spend their money on an insurance policy. But, what do most insurance sales people sell?

They sell insurance!

No wonder the business is so difficult. It doesn't take a Harvard degree to figure it out. If you sell insurance… and know that people don't want to buy insurance… why would you continue to beat your head against the wall trying to sell it?

Consider the way most people shop for auto insurance. They call up a number of insurance companies and ask for a quote. The agent or his or her representative asks what coverage the caller is currently carrying, and gives a quote based on those figures.

The caller then thanks the agent or staff member, and goes to the next number on their list. They keep repeating that scenario until they're convinced that they've found the lowest price… and whichever company comes in lowest gets the business.

But, wait a minute. Isn't there more to buying insurance than just "low price?" Well, sure there is. And you and I both know it. And so do most insurance agents.

Why is it, then, that nearly every agent from nearly every insurance company you call tries to sell on price… knowing that there's probably someone out there with a lower price than they can quote?

Why is it that so few agents try to differentiate themselves from their competition, and change the prospect's base of thinking away from price, and on to other, more important things?

Price is important, don't get me wrong. It's very important. And it carries a lot of weight in a prospect's buying decision.

But it's only one of many factors that a person needs to consider when making their buying decision.

In actuality, there's very little difference in insurance policies issued by any number of insurance companies in the same geographical area.

And likewise, there's usually very little difference in the products or services you sell versus those same types of products or services sold by your competitors.

General overhead costs, utilities, phones, supplies, wages, and product costs are also similar for most companies that sell like products and services.

So, if all those factors... similarity of products and services, overhead costs and product costs... are pretty much the same, the prices charged by each individual business must, out of necessity, be pretty close, as well.

It's true, that one company may, for example, obtain a lower purchase price on their products and as a result, be able to offer a more attractive sales price for a certain period of time, but eventually, things change and the playing field becomes pretty level once again.

There are other factors not to be overlooked such as investment income and tax write-offs or advantages that can play a role in the prices businesses charge for the things they sell.

But overall, all things considered, the prices charged for the goods and services from one company to another similar company are going to be fairly close over the long haul.

The point is, that, no matter what business you're in...

You will never maintain, long-term...
a competitive advantage because
of the products you offer, or
the prices you charge.

As soon as you develop a new product, or offer a new service, it's just a matter of time before your competition latches on to it and offers the exact same thing, or maybe enhances it and offers it for a lower price. And as soon as you lower your prices, your competition can do the same thing.

The marketplace you operate in is so fiercely competitive... so cutthroat... so unforgiving... that you absolutely *must* do something to differentiate yourself from your competition.

If you don't, you'll be relegated to just another "me-too" business, just like all your competitors.

Now... you want to know the good news?

That's how your competitors operate... in a "ME-TOO!" mode.

Just look around. They're all the same. Their businesses all look the same. Their products are all the same. They walk and talk the same. And their advertising all looks like and says the same things as the next guy's. And because they all operate that way and don't know how to change... it gives you a tremendous opportunity!

You see, if they keep on doing what they've always done... they'll keep on getting what they've always got.

But you... if you want to get something different... you've got to be willing to make some changes. And that's what this program is all about. Making changes... changes that will produce real and measurable results in your business.

But, what you'll learn here isn't enough. These ideas and strategies alone, won't work. You've got to take action on them, if you expect anything different than what you're currently getting.

So, make the action commitment now... and let's get started!

Jon Riley "The new definition of insanity is to keep doing what you're doing and expect any result"

Joel and Martin are on the right track and this is just the introduction. You're reading this book for a reason. The reason is to change your

MINDSET!

"Brain cells create ideas. Stress kills brain cells. Stress is not a good idea."
Richard Saunders, aka Poor Richard

Achieving Outstanding Business Success

Personal Traits of Exceptional Performers

Some time back a friend of mine had the pleasant opportunity of having dinner with his friend Earl Nightingale, the famous radio personality and producer of self improvement cassette programs.

Earl made his life's work studying successful people and how they achieved their successes. My friend had long admired Earl for his ideas and philosophy.

And on that occasion, my friend asked him what advice he would give his young son if he had one. What, based on his vast experience and knowledge, would be the one thing that would help his son ensure success both in business as well as in his personal life?

Earl said told my friend, "You know, I have often thought about that very question. And after all the years and all the study, I've come to the conclusion that your success in life, or in business for that matter, can be boiled down to one thing. That is, your rewards will always be in direct proportion to the amount of service you render.

"You only have to look around," he said. "The people who serve others, prosper. The people who don't serve others, don't prosper. And you can tell just how successful a person is by the amount of service they render to others.

"The problem," he continued, "is that unsuccessful people either haven't learned that great secret, or they don't apply it.

"The successful people are the ones who develop the habits of doing the things that unsuccessful people don't do for one reason or another."

What Failures Don't Like to Do

Earl's comments hit my friend like a big hammer that night, as he realized how true they were. The more you serve your customers, and help them satisfy their needs, the more you will prosper.

And as a business owner, business manager, professional person or entrepreneur, serving your customer's needs effectively means that you must do the things that unsuccessful business owners, managers, professionals, and entrepreneurs don't do. The things that those unsuccessful people don't do are the things that most of us don't like to do either.

There is no doubt that it is difficult to work long hours or on weekends when your family is waiting for you at home, and only have a couple of "shoppers" stop by or be stood up for an appointment someone made with you.

It's tough to make telephone calls, only to be met with hostile and rude people on the other end who curse at you or slam the phone down.

It's discouraging to set goals, schedule interviews, explain the technical aspects and benefits of the products and services you provide, overcome customer's objections and misconceptions, and go out of your way to give exceptional service, only to have your customer go elsewhere because they found the same product or service for a few dollars less.

Enough of these experiences can be discouraging for anyone. And after a while, some people just quit trying. They find it easier to adjust their standard of living downward to match their income, than to adjust their income upward to create their desired standard of living.

They are no longer in control. Inflation dictates the price of things they buy, and competition and luck determine how much they have to spend. Fortunately for them, many of their competitors are in the same situation.

Outstanding success is unusual, and is dependent on many different factors. For some people, it just happens. They're in the right place at the right time, they do nothing special, and everything just falls into place for them. Others put in long hours and much work, only to find average success.

But a clear understanding of success principles, a well developed and executed plan, and certain personal traits and characteristics can help move you towards your goals more quickly.

Here are some personal qualities to consider:

Eight Personal Qualities for Success

1. Know What You Want

Know yourself and exactly what you want and expect out of your business. So many people enter into business and spend years in that business environment without having any idea of what they want, or what is possible to get out of their business. And it's no different in the insurance profession.

In fact, most business owners are working so hard *in* their businesses that they don't have time to work *on* them. As a result, they've become slaves to their business. They've got things backwards. They're working for their business rather than their business working for them.

Take the time to carefully analyze where you've come from, where you are now, and what you want to accomplish in your business, your job or your career. Then begin to set some meaningful goals to help you accomplish your objectives. You see, if you don't know where you want to go, you'll have no idea of what to do in order to get there.

Meaningful goals are an essential requirement for success in business. With goals, you have a target to aim for, a purpose for being, and a direction to travel. Without goals, it's easy to wander aimlessly, getting sidetracked with any little thing that comes along.

When you set your goals, think of the word, "SMART." You should have SMART goals. That is, your goals should be:

- Specific,
- Measurable,
- Attainable,
- Realistic, and
- Time-bound

It is important for your goals to be *Specific,* so you will know exactly what you're shooting for. Your goal should be clearly defined and identified so you not only know what you are trying to accomplish, you'll also know when you achieve it.

Just to say you want to sell more products, merchandise or services or reduce the number of contacts to close a sale isn't enough. You need to clearly specify your goal. Is it 12 more sales per month? An extra $100,000 in monthly sales? How about a certain amount of certain types of products or services? How much – specifically?

Whatever your goal, there should be no doubt about what you wish to accomplish.

Your goals should be *Measurable.* That is, there should be a system, or method of determining how you are progressing in your efforts for attainment. By clearly defining your goals as discussed in the previous step, you will be more able to measure them. It's important for you to be able to see your current status, as well as progression towards your goals.

Next, your goals should be *Attainable.* If your goal is too high... if there's no hope for you to reach it, it won't take long for you to become discouraged, and you will either lose concentration and the drive necessary to pursue your goal, or you will abandon it altogether.

Your goal should be something you can reach with just a little extra effort.

An insurance agency owner I'm acquainted with had a large fire and casualty agency. In order to promote the sale of life insurance to his on-board customers, the agency owner introduced a contest for his agents. The agent who sold the most life insurance would win a trip to Hawaii.

One of the agents who worked for the agency but who had never sold much life insurance, decided he wanted to try and win the trip. The qualifications to earn the trip were tough, and were based entirely on the sale of life insurance.

Very few agents in this agency ever earned these types of trips by working the entire year for them, but this particular agent put his mind to it and qualified in only four months.

Considering the agent's past performance with regards to life insurance production, it's questionable whether the goal should have been attainable for him. However, the agent found a motivation within that changed the odds to his favor, and he was able to accomplish in a four month period, what most agents weren't able to do in an entire year.

In your business operation, you need to make sure your goals are not only attainable, but are also...

Realistic. If your goal isn't realistic, that is, if it's not something within your realm of achievement, it's just a matter of time before you'll become frustrated and give up. And that can have a negative effect on you as you begin to think of yourself as a failure, or not being good at setting goals.

Then, because of your negative image of yourself relative to setting goals, you will likely give up setting goals in the future. It's a self-feeding mechanism. The key to being good at setting and achieving goals is to be realistic in your expectations. Set attainable and realistic goals that can be reached with a small amount of effort.

That builds a success image, and enhances your self confidence in a positive way. Then, the next time, set a little higher goal. Not much higher, just a little higher. Again, one that you know you can achieve. And that adds on to, and builds your confidence, that much more.

The next step is to make your goals, *Time-bound.* That is, you should set a time limit for their attainment.

This helps you keep on target, not be distracted, and encourages you to complete something you've started. Not only will this help you to realize success at a pre-designated time, but you will enhance your self image by accomplishing your goal.

If, for instance, your goal is to sell a certain number of a certain type of product or service, or a pre-determined dollar amount of sales this year, break that number down into months, weeks, and even days, if necessary.

A large goal becomes much more manageable in small pieces. The key is to break your goals into bite-size pieces, and place a time deadline on them, for their accomplishment.

2. The Ability to Focus

The second quality is the ability to focus. Many people hesitate to go into business because they think they lack the talents and abilities necessary to succeed. They look at others who are successful and think that they must have unique talents or capabilities. But after getting to know that person, they find them to really be quite average.

The main difference is that the successful person has developed the ability to focus. A person of average intelligence who is focused on a clearly identified and specific goal, will consistently outperform the brightest people who are not focused on anything specific.

3. Determine the Price You'll Pay

You must determine the price you'll have to pay to be successful. For everything in life, there is a price. And it must be paid before you can realize the rewards. In many instances, it takes sacrifice.

A few years ago, in an effort to get a little exercise and help relieve stress, one of my friends bought his wife and himself matching bicycles. They had fun for awhile, but then a group of experienced riders flew by him one day on their fast, shiny, obviously high-priced racing bikes.

Always a competitive person, my friend decided that he would try to catch them and ride with them. But, try as he might, it was to no avail. Nothing he did would allow me to catch up to them. That ate on my friend for about a week, and it wasn't long before he found myself back in the bike shop getting the specifications and prices of one of those "fast, shiny, obviously high-priced" bikes.

$2,500 later, he was back on the road just waiting for those riders to catch him so he could ride with them. My friend was completely decked out in cycling shorts and jersey, special shoes, helmet and his new 16-speed racer.

Then, one day it happened. The group of riders came up on my friend from behind, and he was determined to keep up with them. But a quarter of a mile later, try as he might, he was "off the back." The riders were gone, never to be seen again. That really irritated my friend.

So he bought several books, obtained some video tapes, and sought out the help of a neighbor who was a pretty good rider. He worked hard trying to develop his cycling abilities. He rode every morning from 4:30 to 7:30, while his family was still asleep.

My friend encountered motorists who didn't like cyclists. Some even went so far as to run him off the road and have bottles thrown at him.

He's ridden in the rain and cold weather, and he's ridden in the 120 degree heat. My friend worked hard and eventually hired a cycling coach to help him develop his skills.

Then he entered a local race, and to his surprise he won! This encouraged him so he entered another race. Then another. And another. And he kept winning.

With the new skills and confidence he was developing, he entered the state and national championships, placing very high in both. The riders who used to pass him were now coming to him for help and advice. They wondered how he could consistently beat them when he hadn't been riding for nearly as long as they had.

What they didn't understand was that it wasn't how long my friend had been training, as much as what he had put into his training.

It wasn't what he did during the race that counted as much as it was what he did during the long, lonely, solitary hours of training.

It was the sacrifices he made that made the difference between being a social rider or the national champion he eventually became.

The same concept of sacrifice applies to operating a successful business.

If you want to reap the great and abundant rewards your business can provide you, you're going to have to do some not-so-glamorous things at some not-so-convenient times.

You're going to have to do what Earl Nightingale said… you'll have to do "…the things that unsuccessful business owners don't want to do."

That may mean, depending on the type of business you have or operate, that you'll have to leave the comfort of your store or office to visit with people about their needs in their homes or businesses at inconvenient times.

If you have a family, this may prove to be a hardship on you, but if you are just starting out in business, or want to increase your existing business or achieve some new goals, you may have to make that sacrifice.

If you are not willing to make the necessary sacrifices, then you can't expect to be as successful in business as someone who is willing to make those sacrifices.

4. Self-Responsibility

You are totally responsible for the success of your business and your life. There are no excuses. There may be set-backs or economic down-turns, or problems that affect your business.

Your suppliers or vendors may discontinue making or providing your favorite products or services, change the way they do business with you or even merge with another company.

Economies change, corporate policies change, and prospects don't buy from you, and the weather is too hot or too cold.

While those things definitely have an impact on you, the way you do business and the sales you make, it is important to realize that those things are beyond your control, and it's up to you, and you alone, to accept responsibility for the success of your business.

No matter how bad you might have it, no matter what difficulties or challenges you might encounter, let me assure you that there are many people who have had difficulties and challenges far greater than any you are ever likely to encounter, and somehow, they manage to pull through. And you can do the same.

Here's a little credo that can help you. It contains just ten, two-letter words:

"If it is to be, it is up to me."

That simple one-line sentence says it all. It places the responsibility exactly where it should be... *directly on your shoulders.*

5. Be Committed

Make a total commitment to your success. Once you have made the decision to be in business, be in that business.

Get into it with both feet. Don't let anything hold you back.

Even more than getting in the business, see that the business gets in you.

Make a commitment that you are going to succeed, no matter what.

Don't try to work two different jobs or projects at one time. You can't do either of them justice, and you'll likely end up frustrated and broke, and never know whether or not you could have been successful.

6. The Extra Mile

The sixth personal quality necessary to achieve outstanding success in business is that you must be willing to go the extra mile.

It's the "Under promise, over deliver" concept, and can be summed up in the following statement:

"If you are always willing to do more than what you get paid for, the day will come when you will be paid for more than what you actually do."

Robert Cialdini, in his book, ***Influence: The Psychology of Persuasion***, discusses what he calls the Law of Reciprocity. Basically, it says that when you do something for someone else there's an unstated obligation for them to want to do something for you in return.

So, when you go the extra mile for your customers or clients, you've just set the stage for that law to take effect. But it's only on that "extra mile" that this works. When you give what might be considered "normal" service, or "adequate" service or – even "good" service, you haven't earned the right to expect that law to work for you.

In fact, even performing "knock-out" service often isn't enough to gain you an advantage. We've all come to expect that from any number of businesses.

You've really got to do something special in order to gain an advantage in today's highly competitive marketplace. Then, and only then, can you expect to create that nearly compelling desire in your customer to want to reciprocate. This simple truth says it all:

"There's no traffic jam on the extra mile."

7. Control Your Time

The seventh quality is that you must master and take control of your time. Time is an expendable commodity. Each one of us has the same 24 hours in each day. When those hours are gone, they cannot be replaced. They are gone forever, never to be recaptured.

You must treat your time as precious, and guard it wisely and selfishly. Don't let anyone disrupt you or take you away from the focus you have on your goals.

People who don't have goals are used by people who do. If you let others draw you away from your goals, you are simply saying that their goals are more important than your own.

If you are serious about business success – really serious, then this is one of the most important and critical areas to defend.

8. Persistence and Determination

Number eight, is to develop persistence and determination. From time to time you will encounter set-backs or reach plateaus where it seems like nothing is going right.

Your competitors lower their prices, run massive ad campaigns and unheard-of promotions, and the next thing you know your customers and clients begin doing business with them.

Business is walking out the back door faster than it's coming in the front door.

Your volume is beginning to drop, and you become concerned.

You seem to be spending more time in a defensive posture than you do in servicing your existing customers, and you're losing.

Now is not the time to give up. Now is the time to dig in and begin to play offensively.

To be determined not to lose your good customers – the ones you worked so hard to get. Your strategy should be to keep in touch with them and continue providing exceptional service.

Nearly every business is cyclical. Eventually things will change.

While you can't be competitive on price all the time, you can be competitive on the service you give, and the empathy you have for your customers and their problems.

We'll talk more about how to do that in a later chapter, but for now, just resolve in advance; that no matter what, you'll never give up.

Six Personal Abilities Help Guarantee Results

In addition to those eight personal qualities, there are there are six additional abilities that can help you achieve even greater success:

1. Effective Communication

First, is the ability to communicate effectively with others. You must be able to interact with other people on their level, so they understand you and the points you are trying to get across to them.

Remember that everyone is different. Each of us have different communication and behavior styles, and you need to be versatile enough to relate to each person according to their individual style. Be careful that you speak language that they are familiar with and can relate to, and that you don't overuse "buzz words," or industry jargon.

2. Stay on Target

This is the ability for you to quickly make midstream corrections. Each one of us is human, and are subject to the frailties that accompany this mortal life. From time to time, we all make mistakes or errors in judgment.

Making the mistake or the error is not the problem – the first time. It's when we keep making the same mistakes over and over again, without learning from them, or that we fail to quickly recover and make the necessary corrections to avoid total calamity, that we run into problems.

3. Develop Foresight

The ability to spot and analyze trends. To be able to look at the past as well as what is happening today, and predict what might happen in the future, can have a significant impact on your business success. Another word for this skill is "foresight."

In a recent interview, the president of a very large meat company told how just a few years ago, their largest selling items were canned hams. But today, with more women working, and less time to spend in the kitchen, they sell very few canned hams.

Today their mainstay is precooked dinners. Without foresight, or the ability to look ahead and predict with reasonable accuracy what may happen in the near future, a company could lose its competitive position and find itself in serious trouble.

As a business owner, you should give serious thought to keeping abreast of industry changes, new laws, tax laws, buying trends, and other factors that could affect your customers either positively or negatively. Then take whatever steps are necessary to prepare yourself to address those changes, as well as posture yourself in the minds of your customers as the expert they've come to know and depend on.

4. Demonstrate Leadership

The fourth ability or skill to develop for outstanding success is that of leadership. Leadership is the ability to take charge and move others to action.

When you are working with a prospect, client or customer, and have identified and analyzed their needs, it is up to you to prepare and recommend a good, workable plan or proposal that will help satisfy those needs; a plan that's right for their situation and that fits their budget.

It's not up to the customer to tell you what they want. You are the professional. They have come to you for help and advice. You've got a lot more experience, knowledge and understanding of your products and services and what they can do for them than they do. It is up to you to take charge and assume responsibility for the satisfaction and solving of their problems, needs and wants.

And if you approach it with the right mix of professionalism, knowledge and confidence you'll be amazed at how many people will take your advice and follow your leadership.

5. Persuasive Selling Skills

The ability to sell well. It's surprising how little most people in business know about professional selling. Selling is one of the most important skills you as a professional business person can possess.

Many of your prospects and your existing customers know just enough about what your products or services can do for them to be dangerous. They have talked to other people, read a few articles in some magazines, may even have seen a program or two on television, checked things out on the Internet, and they think they know exactly what they need. In some cases, they may be close.

But in other cases, they're far from the mark. You owe it to your customers to be as effective a salesperson as you can be. By doing that, you'll end up giving those better solutions and better value, saving them both time and money, and helping them have greater piece of mind knowing they have the products or services that are best for them.

They will also feel good about their choice of a place of business, knowing that they have just dealt with real professionals who really care about them.

You will be a beneficiary of that effort, too. You will you feel good about yourself and the job you have just done for your customer, and that will cause you to be more effective and professional in your next interview or sale. Not only that, but your customer, being satisfied with what you have done for him or her, will be more inclined to tell others of their experience.

Believe me, people respond to the personal experiences of people they respect. And they'll respond to you, because a real professional and caring person or business is hard to find these days.

6. Action

The sixth ability to develop is that of action. All the things we've discussed in this chapter will do you, nor anyone else (your customers, for instance) any good if you don't take action and do something about them.

Remember, action is the key. As we discussed earlier, it's not what you know, it's not what you talk about, it's what you do. True success in business, or in life, is an ongoing process. As my friend, Joel Weldon says,

"The Road to Success is Always
Under Construction."

Some people say that knowledge is power. But it isn't. Knowledge is not power unless it's applied. This chapter has supplied you with some vital knowledge necessary to be successful in business. You now have the knowledge – now it's up to you to put that knowledge into action.

Jon Riley *"There is no traffic on that extra mile".* This sums up the whole chapter and the book. Hardly anyone goes the extra mile. That is why there really is little to no competition. *"You are only in completion with yourself".* Applied Knowledge is Power and **Perfect Practice makes Permanent.** Now let's dive into my favorite subject:

CUSTOMERS!

"Laughter is the shortest distance between two people."
Victor Borge

How Do Your Customers See You?

Establishing a Positive Identity in the Minds of Your Customers

Think of the word, "Professional." What image comes to your mind? Do you visualize a doctor, a dentist, a lawyer, or perhaps the president of a large corporation?

Did the image of the owner or manager of the business you operate cross your mind?

What criteria do you use to define a "professional?"

What about other people – your customers, for example?

How do you think they define a "professional?"

The services you perform for your customers on a daily basis, can have a big impact on them, their family, their staff, employees or customers if they have businesses, and their financial futures.

The way you run your business and handle your customers' needs on a daily basis says a lot about you and the position you occupy in their minds.

In truth, your occupation should be viewed as being just as "professional" as that of any other, including doctors, dentists, lawyers, or any other type of business head.

The critical question is, how professionally do you perform within the scope of your occupation?

While this program is not a sales training course, it's important to know that no matter what your role in business is, you're involved in sales in one form or another.

And if you have staff or employees who are involved in sales, it's important for you to know the following information.

Five Types of Salespeople

Just as different salespeople have their own different and unique personalities, they also have different skill levels when it comes to selling and servicing their customers.

As we discuss the various types of salespeople and classify them according to their skill level, you will no doubt recognize some of the people you know or have encountered in the past. And as we do, take an honest look at yourself, to see where you might fit.

Professional Visitor

This person doesn't have any problem making appointments. In fact, they thrive on it. They enjoy visiting and talking to people, getting to know them, and may even engage in a casual discussion of their customers' problems.

Their conversation with a customer or prospect may or may not eventually involve the subject of how their products or services can benefit the buyers, and if it does, it usually has to be instigated by the customer or prospect.

A typical sales presentation will be oral, with very little (if any) use of visual materials, product brochures, or printed proposals.

Order Taker

These people don't mind talking to customers, clients or prospects, if they don't have to initiate the call. They are uncomfortable making appointments, and would rather have the customer or prospect come to them.

The telephone presents just as much a problem for these people. If the phone rings, they'll take the call and even discuss the customer's needs. But it's tough for them to pick up the receiver and dial a customer's number.

They operate best from a base of "low-price," and have difficulty handling objections. They would rather wait until someone asks for something specific, then they have no trouble filling the order.

Peddler

These are "sales-oriented" people. They have good product knowledge, but severely lack in "people skills." They operate from a sort of "hit-and-run" approach.

This person will assume a certain level of product knowledge on the part of the customer, and spend very little, if any, time establishing rapport with them. These people are either "product-oriented," or "price-oriented." Their entire presentation is based on product features or price, with little regard to how the product or service will benefit the customer.

The Peddler is the most prevalent type of salesperson you will find. Telemarketers who work the consumer market fit nicely into this category. It seems like it never fails. You may have just gotten home from a tough day at work and are relaxing with the kids, working in the yard, or perhaps even eating dinner.

Then the phone rings. It's for you. The person on the other end dives right into their presentation with no regard for the person they're calling.

For most people, especially professional salespeople, this inconvenience and the salesperson's level of incompetence is most aggravating. In these types of calls, the salesperson shows no concern for the prospect's time, inconvenience, present level of product knowledge, or whether or not there's any level of need, want or desire to know more about what they're selling.

The assumption is made by the caller that what he or she is offering the prospect in terms of a product, service or convenience is the same or better than what the prospect currently has, and that all the prospect is interested in is price. This type of approach is an insult to the prospect or customer, and is one of the biggest mistakes a salesperson can make.

Problem-Solver

These are salespeople who enjoy getting in front of people, ferreting out problems, needs and wants, and discussing workable solutions. They have empathy for the customer, can see the customer's needs *from the customer's point of view,* and enjoy helping the customer solve their problems.

The problem-solving person is good at establishing rapport with the prospect or customer, identifying what their needs, wants and desires are, developing creative, needs and wants-satisfying proposals, and making effective presentations.

But when it comes time to ask for the order, or close the sale, they tense up, lose their confidence, or otherwise fail to close the sale. Their customers or prospects, now having their needs identified and solutions presented, go elsewhere looking for a "better buy."

This salesperson has done all the work, and an Order-Taker for another company gets the sale – and the commission. After the Peddler, this is the next most common type of salesperson.

Counselor

In the business world, it's not uncommon for companies and corporations to have a staff of lawyers, or "legal counsel," on retainer to give advice in matters pertaining to the law, taxes, investments, mergers, or other difficult or legal situations.

The Counselor knows that when it comes to important buying decisions, his or her customers, be they companies, corporations, or individuals, should be no different.

To them, buying any type of product or service is a serious matter, not to be taken lightly, and can be an important tool for solving a need, satisfying a problem or adding to their profits, convenience or lifestyle.

They know that their customers need professional and qualified representation and advice, and the Counselor will do whatever it takes to provide it for them.

Like corporate legal counsel, this salesperson postures him or herself as being "on retainer," always available to give advice on matters pertaining to the products or services they sell. They make it clear in the customer's mind that there is absolutely no need for them to go anywhere else for answers to the problems their products or services can solve.

The Counselor knows how to establish rapport, build professional trust and credibility, identify their customer's current problems, develop effective proposals, offer credible and workable solutions, and make the presentation in such a way that their customers have no question in their minds but that they must buy the concepts they present, and hence, the product or service.

In addition, they have the ability to point out other, potential problems that the customer might encounter, and help them solve those needs as well.

This person operates much like a professional billiards champion. Before each shot, the billiards champion will carefully analyze the layout of the balls on the table, to see where the next two or three shots can best be made.

Then, with precision, he makes the shot at hand, and skillfully directs the cue ball to a predetermined spot so it is poised for the next shot.

Salespeople who function at this skill level also carefully review the customer's needs, both stated and unstated, and skillfully set in motion, a plan to address those needs either now, or at a later, more convenient date.

Objections rarely come up because the Counselor has taken the time to anticipate what objections may arise, and then build the answers to the potential objections into his or her presentation.

This salesperson will get every drop of business the customer has, not because of price, but because the customer knows the salesperson really cares about them, understands their needs, and is willing to take the time to identify those needs and offer workable and credible solutions.

How Do Your Customers See You?

How do your customers see you? I mean, when the people you deal with on a regular basis, your customers and prospects — when they view you as the person they do, or are considering doing business with, who do they see?

Are you someone they might classify as a "typical salesperson" — someone who is out to sell them another product or service, or who is interested more in the sale or commission they'll earn?

Or do your customers and prospects view you more as a counselor — someone they like and can relate to and who is genuinely interested in them, and making sure they have the right product for their individual and specific needs, at the best possible price? And in the event that what they've purchased does not, or will not work for them, or if you're not satisfied for any reason, will be behind you making things right?

How you answer this basic and important question is critical to your success in business. It can mean the difference between enormous success, mediocrity, or even dismal failure.

And, it's a self-feeding mechanism, as well. If you are viewed by your customers as a time waster or a product-hustler, even if it is not stated, you will tend to pick up that message yourself, and act accordingly, thus reinforcing your customer's image of you.

On the other hand, if your customers welcome you as a counselor, or an advisor — someone with their best interests in mind — someone who can help them identify and solve their problems, they will feel good about you. And consequently, you will also feel good about yourself, and the role you play relative to your customer. You will be and act more professional, more confident, and will be better able to help your customer with the solving of his or her needs and problems.

As you fill the role as a problem solver, you can't help but reinforce and strengthen that positive image in both you, and your customer's minds.

What Your Customers Really Want

As a business person, it is important for you to understand that only 35% of the reason people buy the products or services you offer, is for the actual product or service itself.

The other 65% of the reason they buy, is for what you can do or provide for your customer beyond the product or service, and what that product or service does for the customer.

In other words, if you are trying to sell your customers and prospects *products and services*, you are wasting your time. They are only 35% interested in *products and services.*

But they are 65% interested in the benefits of *having you involved.*

You see, chances are good that your customers and prospects can buy the same product or service (or at least comparable ones) from any one of several of your competitors.

And with that product or service, your competitor may offer a number of additional advantages, as well.

They may have a lower price, better quality product, some added bonuses or extra services, a location that's more convenient, or a payment plan that fits their budget better.

In today's tough, competitive market, it's difficult to compete on price or product. You may be able to command a certain advantage for a period of time because you have a lower price than your competitors, but you and I both know that it will be short-lived.

The truth is, you will never be able to maintain a competitive position in the marketplace – long-term for any length of time because of the prices you charge or the products you provide.

It'll just be a matter of time before either one of your competitors lowers their prices or duplicates (or even betters) your product, or you raise your prices because you no longer have the necessary margins to justify your prices.

But there's one thing your customers can't get from any of your competitors. And that's you, and the empathy, the problem solving expertise and the knowledge, education and commitment to service that you bring to his or her specific and unique situation.

Products and Services, or Advice?

So, it is important to continually ask yourself (and be honest) the following question…

"How do your customers… the people
who do business with you… your
clients and prospects, see you?"

On the next page is an example of an easy method you can use to find out.

Take a sheet of paper and draw a line down the middle.

On the left-hand side at the top, label the column, "Products and Services."

Label the right-hand column, "Help and Advice."

Every time you are in contact with a customer or prospect, whether they call you or you have a face-to-face meeting, evaluate the overall purpose of the meeting.

Products and Services	Help and Advice
| | | | | | | | | | | | | |	| | | | | | | | | | | | | | | | | | | | | | | | | | | | | | | | | | | | | | |

Did your customer or prospect look to you for the products or services you provide? Or did they seek your help, advice or counsel to help them make a decision that would solve a particular need or challenge they were encountering?

Once you've determined that, place a mark in the appropriate column. Then at the end of the month, evaluate the results of your list.

If you have more marks in the "Products and Services" column than in the "Help and Advice" column, you pretty well know what perception your customers have of you.

But equally important, you also know what you need to do to change that perception. You can then begin to develop and implement a plan of action that focuses on improving your image in the eyes of your customers. Then test yourself again several months later. By comparing your evaluation sheets over the period of a year or two, you can easily see the progress you're making.

Improvement is not always difficult. Oftentimes, a person may not know where they are weak or where they need to improve. But if you can isolate those areas that need improvement, you can then begin to take the necessary steps to effect positive change.

Jon Riley "**If you are early, you are on time**". If you are on time you are late and if you are late you are incompetent. Arriving to a job early generates referrals. I have not advertised in over 20 years and I have "**Consistent Customers**" and you can too. Just keep learning.

Next is the 3 keys to success and who really is:

THE BOSS

3 How Much Are You Worth?

Strategies for Determining and Increasing Your Value to Your Customers

You are in business for yourself. That is, you may own your own business, or you may be associated with another company or firm, either as an employee, a partner or an independent contractor. Your working agreement or arrangement doesn't really matter.

The important thing to realize is that no matter what the arrangement or situation you presently find yourself in, you are really working for yourself. If you work by commission, for example, the sales you make are not only putting dollars in your employer's pocket, they are putting dollars into your own pocket, as well. The more you sell, the more you make.

Just consider yourself as a business that prospers or falters financially by the amount of commission dollars you generate. The point is, even though you may be working for, or associated with another company or concern, you are really working for yourself to increase the amount of money you earn for you.

Three Keys for Success

It's important to realize that your success in whatever you do in business, or in life, for that matter, will always be determined by three things:

1. The need or demand for what you do,

2. Your ability to do it, and
3. The difficulty in replacing you.

In other words, how valuable are you and the service you perform, to other people?

To illustrate this point, let's apply our 3-step formula to the job of an elevator operator. In today's world of pushbutton, self-operated elevators, how much need is there for the job he or she performs?

Most people are quite capable of operating an elevator themselves. It doesn't take much knowledge or training, so an operator can be replaced without much difficulty. As a result, elevator operators, if you can even find one, are not paid much.

Now, contrast the elevator operator and the money he or she commands with that of a professional major league baseball player. Specifically, a player that is good at batting.

What is the *need for what they do?* A look at attendance figures for baseball games will show that more than just a few fans are interested in watching what they do. So the need obviously is great.

How about the batter's *ability to do what he does?* Sports analysts say that the action of hitting a ball moving towards you at over 90 miles per hour is the single most difficult movement in sports.

In the game of basketball, the target (the hoop) doesn't move. Same in golf. While the ball moves, the hole, or goal, remains stationary. In football, there are 11 teammates all with a common goal of advancing the ball. But in baseball, it's the batter alone, trying to hit a small, 90 M.P.H. target with his bat. So it stands to reason then, that the better or more often a batter can hit the ball, the more he or she will be compensated.

Now, what about the *difficulty in replacing* a good batter? When only the best in the world can hit the target less than a third of the time, and most of the other players are successful far less than that, it doesn't take long to realize why the best batters are among the highest moneymakers in the world.

Obtaining Superior Rewards

Now how about you? It's been said that you can tell how professional a person is by the size of their income at the end of the year.

And you can tell exactly how valuable the service you perform is by how much people are willing to pay you for it. If you do the same job that everybody else does, and do it no better than the way they do it, you can't expect to earn more money, or be considered any more valuable than those other people.

You see, the market, by nature, will pay superior rewards only for superior goods and services. It will pay average rewards for average goods and services, and it will see that inferior rewards are paid for inferior goods and services.

In other words, you will be rewarded in direct proportion to the value you provide your customers. It's inescapable. That's the law of nature.

Now, if the products and services you sell or provide are similar in coverage and price to everyone else's (and most of them are, today), then the difference between you and other people in your position has to be in the type and amount of personal service you provide your customers and clients.

This, then, has to be the area you excel in – it becomes your competitive edge.

Guaranteeing Business Success

So, one of the main keys to success in business, then, is, number one, to make sure that there is a great *need or demand for what you do.*

One of the best ways to guarantee that is to make sure you only spend your time selling to qualified prospects. That is, people who need, want and can pay for what you're selling. There may be people who need or want what you have, but if they can't afford to pay for it, or if you can't arrange suitable payment options for them, you'll spend a seemingly endless amount of time and get nowhere.

On the other hand, there may be people who have the ability to pay, but not the need or want. In these cases, you can also waste considerable time, because surely, no sale will result from your efforts.

The second point is that you are paid in direct proportion to your *ability to do what it is that you do.* That is, to identify, qualify and sell the products and services you offer to your prospects and customers, and then service their needs as they arise.

In some businesses, the sole function of salespeople is to seek out qualified prospects and sell them the products or services offered by the business. The necessary service work for the customer is provided by an office or support staff.

In other businesses, each salesperson is responsible in every way for each of their customer's needs, from the initial sale, to providing all the necessary service the customer might require, including updating the product or service, customer complaints, changes of address, or any other service work that may be needed.

The determining factor then, is not what your responsibilities are, but rather, how good you are at performing those responsibilities.

Third, remember, that you are paid in direct proportion to the difficulty *in replacing you.*

When I think of this area, I think of Disneyland and Disneyworld. As attractions go, they have very little competition. And as far as theme parks? They are unsurpassed. Their average daily attendance figures bear this out.

Disneyland - California 44,398
Disneyworld, Epcot Center – Florida ... 30,767
Disneyland - Tokyo 47,161

With 122,326 guests visiting each day, and paying an average of $98 per person, the Disney properties are light years ahead of their nearest competition. And, why? Because they have met the criteria outlined in the 3-step formula.

Let's consider each of the steps of the formula as they apply to Disney.

First, is there a need for what they do? Certainly there must be.

Entertainment is the largest and fastest growing business in the world today, both in terms of participants, and in total dollar revenue.

Next, how about Disney's ability to do what they do? With over 44 million people visiting their 3 parks each year, evidence would indicate that they are doing at least a few things, if not a whole lot of things right.

And finally, the difficulty in replacing them? Nothing has come close yet, and with those 44 million people spending over $4.3 billion, odds are that the people who visit the Disney properties are pretty satisfied.

The Law of Unlimited Abundance

Walt Disney was a man of extraordinary vision and foresight. He knew what it would take to be successful in his chosen area of business, and he developed a formula that expressed his philosophy, and could be used in any type of business to ensure its success. He called it, his "Law of Unlimited Abundance."

Walt said that it didn't matter what type of business or endeavor a person was engaged in, they could be successful and enjoy *unlimited abundance*, if they would simply follow his formula or plan.

Walt Disney's "Law of Unlimited Abundance," stated, that to be successful, you must,

"Do what you do so well, that the people who see you do it, will want to see you do it again, and will bring others to see you do it."

That's the credo that built the enormous successes of Disneyland and Disneyworld. And in their arena of operation, they stand alone.

Disney's Law Can Work for You!

It can be similar in your business world, too. You see, the key is to, "*do what you do*," not what someone else does, but what *you* do. You don't have to copy. You simply do your job the way only you can. That's what makes you special, sets you apart from others, and attracts people to you.

Then you do what you do, "*so well*," that is, provide the type of service your customers require, want, or need in an exceptional manner. It leaves no room for mediocrity, it's "so well." That implies exceptional performance.

And if you will do that so, "*the people who see you do it*," (your customers), "*will want to see you do it again*," (that's repeat business), "*and will bring others to see you do it*," (that's referral business), you too, can meet with an unparalleled success.

Because so few people perform in business that way, it sets you completely apart from all the competition. Customers can't get the kind of service you offer from anyone or anywhere else. It's simply not available anywhere, at any price.

So, by default, you become unique, different, and difficult to replace. And it will be reflected in your business and your income. It has to. There's no choice. It is a basic, eternal law of nature. You simply reap the results of what you've sown.

You Reap What You Sow

The question you must answer in your mind is, "What are you going to sow, so you will reap the kinds of rewards you wish to have?"

In the world of business, this is a most critical question, and one you would do well to take the time to answer. Fact is, most business people simply don't understand how important the answer to this one question really is.

You see, many people go into business because it is something they have always wanted to do, or because they want a certain amount of freedom, or perhaps they want to be their own boss.

Now, those are not necessarily bad reasons, but they are selfish reasons for the most part, and while they may sound good on the surface, in actuality, some of them may not be very practical.

If you go into business for selfish reasons, and fail to give the customer his or her rightful due, your chances of success are likely to meet with hard times.

Business, like farming, requires that you do certain things in a particular order if you are to realize an abundant harvest. Now the answer to the question,

**"What are you going to sow,
so you will reap the kinds of rewards you want?"**

…is simple. You only have to look at the question backwards. First, what kinds of rewards do you want? Second, what do you have to do to get those rewards? And third, who is it that can give you those rewards?

If you will always remember that although you may own or work for, or represent, a certain company or organization, they are not who pays you.

The Customer Signs Your Paycheck

It really is the customer that signs your paycheck. And although you must see that your company's interests are always considered, you must not lose sight that the customer is the boss.

They are the whole reason your job exists in the first place. They hire you to help them make good personal and business decisions. They trust you to help them see that their problems or needs are solved or satisfied in an efficient and cost-effective manner, and they pay you well to do your job. It is the wants, needs and desires of your customers that should determine all of your business activity. So the next logical step then, is to learn and understand just what your customer's wants, needs and desires are. And you find that out simply by interviewing and asking them. It is very important to listen carefully to what they say because sometimes there may be other, hidden or unstated wants or needs that may not be readily evident. And only by fully understanding their needs, can you be of meaningful service to them.

Jon Riley. "Creating Customers for life" This could have easily been the book title. You meet a suspect, turn them into a prospect, a prospect into a customer and a customer into a friend who becomes a referral mechanism for life. That is the goal of your new small business. **You want your customers raving about you** to everyone. It will happen when you show up early every time & solve their problem. This is when you take out your recording device, cell phone or tiny pocket camera with a video option and simply ask them, *"How have I made a difference in your life"*. Get an on-camera testimonial. Before you turn off record, ask them if you have permission to use it. Explain that it will enable you to help more people. You can also do a small job free of charge in exchange for a testimonial. In Step One of my **"Your Business Within"** process, I show you how to get your starter testimonials to use on your Free Website.

www.YourBusinessWithin.com

Go there for more info and to apply to my **Serve2Succeed Small Business Academy**, where I select a handful of Mentees and guide them for 90 days of personal coaching working specifically on them and their immediate needs.
It is now time for:

WHY PEOPLE BUY?

"Life is a series of problems. Do we want to moan about them or solve them?"
M. Scott Peck

Why People Buy

Identifying the Basic Motives That Make Your Customers Want To Buy

People don't buy for the sake of owning a certain product or service. Rather, they buy because of the benefits they will receive as a result of owning that product or service.

The example that has traditionally been used to illustrate this point is that one year, a quarter of a million quarter-inch drills were sold, and not one person that bought a drill wanted a quarter-inch drill. Instead, they bought the drills because they wanted the benefits the drill could provide... a hole.

People buy your products and services for the same reason... not for a hole... but for the benefits those products or services provides. Ask the next 10 prospects you come in contact with if they want to buy the product or service you're selling, and chances are, you'll receive a negative answer.

There are many factors that influence people to react that way, and each person has his or her own reasons for doing so. Regardless of individual reasons, it's a fact that people don't want to buy *products*, and they often resent people trying to sell them.

People Buy for the Benefits

On the other hand, if you ask the same person that previously turned you down if they want the specific benefits, the products or services you're selling will provide them, you will most likely receive a positive answer. They may give you a hard time about the prices you are charging, but in most cases, the answer will be a "yes."

Like the quarter-inch drills, people are not interested in products, but they are interested in the benefits the products will provide them. It makes sense then, that when you are making a presentation, that you don't emphasize *products.*

Rather, you should talk in terms of *specific benefits,* and how those benefits apply directly to the particular prospect in front of you at the time.

As mentioned previously, each person is different, and each person has his or her own reasons for buying or not buying. And each person will buy for his or her own reasons – not yours or anyone else's.

If you try to sell them for any reason other than their own, you run the risk of turning them off or otherwise alienating them, which usually ends up destroying the sale you are trying to make, as well as any future sales.

Trying to figure out why people make certain decisions can be a complicated, even frustrating process, at best. But an understanding of basic buying motives can make your job much easier.

Motives for Buying

Behavioral psychologists tell us there are seven basic motives that move a person to action – that cause them to buy. An understanding of these motives and how they apply to your customers and prospects at the time a buying decision is being made, can give you a tremendous advantage.

1. Desire for Gain or Profit

Nobody likes to lose. People want something in return for their efforts and hard work. And the easier they can get it, the better. The success of the lottery games in various states bear testimony of people trying to find an easy way to get gain and profit.

The products you sell can help your customers realize their dreams for gain or profit, too. Your customers can and will invest in various types of products or services you sell – not to own them, per se, but in an effort to increase their profitability and the amount and value of their assets.

2. Fear of Loss, or Need For Security

People will go to great lengths to prevent losing something. In an effort to protect their property, some people install burglar or fire alarms, smoke detectors, or night lights that automatically come on when movement is detected.

Some people carry spray cans of mace, or tear gas, while others have resorted to carrying guns or other weapons to protect their person. Psychologists say that the fear of loss or the need for security is perhaps, the greatest of all the motives.

If the products and services you sell can help protect your clients, their families or their businesses from loss, or if you can in someway increase their security, either at the present time or sometime in the future, you owe it to them to capitalize on that fact as much and as often as possible.

3. Pride of Ownership, Or Status

People want to be noticed and recognized. Little boys ride bicycles with no hands, and little girls dress up and act out dance routines and shout to their parents, "Watch me! Watch me!"

Adults do the same things, but in different ways. While they may not verbally shout out, they still say "Watch me! Watch me!" just as loudly.

They do it by the kinds of cars they drive, the clothes and jewelry they wear, the houses they live in, and the material things they possess.

While people may buy because of the benefits, they like others to see the actual product. In some cases, it's just another way to say, "Watch me!

4. An Interest in Doing Something Easier or More Efficiently

We all want methods of doing things easier. One only has to look around his or her home to notice the abundance of time and/or money-saving conveniences we all enjoy.

What about your products or services?

Do they somehow make a person's job, or a business' way of doing things easier or more efficient?

And if they do, what are the direct and indirect benefits to your prospect or customer?

Is this something you can capitalize on?

5. The Desire for Excitement or Pleasure

A popular bumper sticker states,

"He who dies with the most toys wins."

That message is a clear indication that people want excitement and pleasure. And it seems to suggest that pleasure comes in the "having," rather than in the "getting." It's whomever has the most at the end that wins.

But in reality, "excitement" and "pleasure," for most people comes in the acquiring of things.

Think back about the times you have worked hard to get something, and how excited you were in the process.

But then, once you had whatever it was that you were working for, how the excitement was dulled.

Sometimes it's not the end result that counts as much as the process of acquiring.

A more practical interpretation of the bumper sticker might read,

"He who lives with the most toys wins!"

Of course, these applications have to do with "things." Some people really enjoy acquiring "things," and even keep score by how much they accumulate.

Other people gain great pleasure or excitement knowing that their family's future educational and livings needs, as well as retirement will be taken care of.

Business owners like to know that their businesses are operating at peak efficiency and profitability, and are meeting the needs of their customers, and as a result, will be around for a long-time providing jobs and security for their employees and their families, as well as providing retirement funds for the owner when the business is sold.

6. Self-Improvement or an Increase in Effectiveness

Your investment of both money and time in this course is a good example of your desire for self-improvement and increased effectiveness. People want and need to improve and to be able to do things more efficiently.

Sometimes that involves taking risks with time or money. Not all risks have to be "risky." Calculated risks based on well thought-out plans and outcomes are the safest way to go, and can contribute greatly to the successful improvement in effectiveness and efficiency.

7. The Desire for Importance or the Need to Feel Appreciated

According to noted psychiatrist Dr. Abraham Maslow, this is one of the basic needs of all humans; acceptance and appreciation. Children want to be accepted by their parents and peers, and parents want their children to remember them when they grow up and leave home.

In his book, *The Human Side of Enterprise,* Douglas McGregor explains that workers are motivated more by "significant works," and a feeling of being needed and appreciated, than by money.

People want to make a difference, and be appreciated for it. Fathers and mothers not only have an obligation to see that their family's futures are provided for, but they want their family to understand and appreciate their efforts.

Business owners have an obligation to the people who buy from them, the employees who work for them, their employees' families, the suppliers and the vendors who sell to them. Too often, each of those groups of people live with an attitude of expectancy and entitlement. That is, they expect that the business owner will take care of them. How much better it would be if more appreciation would be shown to those who make our lives better.

If the products or services you provide the marketplace can help make this possible, you may have an open ticket to success because of the great unsatisfied need that exists.

If you understand these basic motives and how they apply to your business of selling your products and services, and then sell to the needs (both stated and unstated) of your customers and prospects, you will prosper.

And if you are not prospering, it simply means you are have not uncovered your prospect's and customer's motives for buying. You are not addressing their specific needs. In most cases you can't wait for your customers to tell you what they want. You have to be able to recognize their needs.

Remember, you are ultimately responsible for the success or failure of your business. If you are doing it right or wrong, either way, the marketplace will let you know.

The Loyalty of the Customer

Customers make an interesting study. It seems that they always want the very most for the very least they'll have to pay. They are ruthless, selfish, demanding and disloyal.

You know the story. You've done business with someone for several years and they've been good customers. You've given them the best service possible and you think they are your customers for life. But then some little thing possibly out of your control goes wrong, or they see an ad or get a call from a competitor, someone they've never met before, with a slightly lower price, and the next thing you know, they are gone, oftentimes without a single word to you.

At first you don't notice it. But one day you realize that it's been a while since you've seen or heard from that customer. When you find out what happened, you feel badly, because if they would have just called you, you might have been able to make a couple of changes and save the business. But it's too late, they're gone.

This scenario is repeated time and again with businesses owners from every company, who sell every type of product or service. It is going to happen. To pretend that it doesn't, or won't happen, is simply deceiving yourself.

It's incredible how many business owners just write off the loss of a good customer. But that's not the thing you should do. Instead, now is the time to become even more proactive and go after that "lost" customer.

One of the best ways to minimize or cut down on the frequency of losing your good customers is to resell them on the reasons they bought from you in the first place. Regularly scheduled meetings or conversations with your customers to remind them of their motives can go a long way in helping insulate your business from the competition.

Remember, that your competition has similar products, services and prices. Also remember that your customer's reasons for buying are only 35 percent based on those products, services, and prices. The other 65 percent is for what you can do for them.

Spend the time with them. Review their needs, wants and concerns. Remind them why they bought from you in the first place. Reinforce their motives, and their decisions for buying, and you will reduce your customer defection rate and develop not only loyal customers, but friends, as well.

Jon Riley. "**They buy from you because of your actions & results**". You show up early & you provide the best service. You are organized and efficient. You don't over react and you stay calm and solve problems. Admit when you are wrong and take a loss if needed. **The Customer is not always right** and you cannot please everyone. I have dismissed several customers over the years. Every time I lost one, I gained another one or two. Do not allow difficult people to rent space in your mind. You have a conditional relationship with your customers. It must be a good healthy working relationship for it to work.

You are now living your life by design and not by default.

"In every difficult situation is potential value. Believe this, then begin looking for it."
Norman Vincent Peale

The Main Purpose of Your Business

Getting and Keeping Customers...Profitability Is Priority Number One

When you have an effective system that will allow you to *profitably* get and keep *quality* customers that will return to do business with you over and over again, and then actively and enthusiastically refer you to others, your business will produce more profits than you can possibly imagine. And then everything else falls into place.

On the other hand, if you don't have enough customers buying from you or using your services regularly, then you'll not likely stay in business for very long, and will never have the chance to make a profit.

Now, let's take a minute and look closely at the individual components of this important business skill…

Knowing How to Profitably Attract Quality Customers

Customers are the lifeblood of any business. Without customers buying the products and services you have to offer, you wouldn't have a business to begin with. But customers alone, aren't enough.

You want *quality* customers… customers who are pleasant to deal with. Customers who return to repurchase from you again and again. Customers who you can sell to and realize a reasonable profit from.

And you want to be able to *profitably* attract them. In other words, the return you realize from your investment of advertising or marketing dollars to acquire new customers, should be positive. You want a positive

R.O.I., or return on your investment.

Next, you want to...

Ethically Exploit Their Maximum Financial Potential

Each of your customers has certain needs and wants. And the more of those needs and wants you can handle for them, the more benefits you can provide them, and the more profits you'll realize.

It should be your goal to sell as many products and services to your customers as they need.

You shouldn't take advantage of them or your relationship with them, but you should make every effort to sell them everything that you can *ethically* justify selling them.

It really comes down to this, and I'll speak very frankly. If you really do provide the best products and services in the marketplace (if you don't, you'd better rethink your ethics and why you're in business), and if you really are the business who can serve your customers' needs better than anyone else (and if you're not, you either need to become that business or get out of the business), then you have a moral and an ethical responsibility to make sure that every one of your customers at least has the opportunity to take advantage of them.

And you should do everything in your power that's *reasonable* and *ethical* to give them that opportunity.

Next you want to...

Convert Your Customers to Advocates Who Actively and Enthusiastically Refer You to Others

By definition, an "advocate" is someone who is a backer, a supporter, a promoter, a believer, an activist, a campaigner, a sponsor.

The last thing you need is a database full of one-product, or one-service customers who buy the minimum amount from you, complain about your prices every time they make a purchase, and give the rest of their business to the company or business who has the lowest prices or a "better deal."

There's no way you can make a profit on these types of customers. Besides, they make your life miserable and drive you crazy in the process.

Who you want are customers who not only give you all (or the majority) of their business, but re-buy from you repeatedly, year after year. You want customers that are so happy and so pleased with what you do for them that they actively and enthusiastically campaign for you. That the story they tell about you is so compelling that the people they tell are nearly forced to call you and ask for your help. Those are the people who make your job fun, enjoyable and profitable.

And finally, you want to…

Keep Your Customers for Life

Reliable studies demonstrate that the more needs a business handles for a customer, the longer they can expect that customer to do business with them.

In the insurance business for instance, an agent increases his chances of keeping an insured for three years or more by the following percentages:

- 45% if the agent insures only the auto policies
- 50% if both the auto and homeowners policies are insured
- 60% with auto, homeowners and life policies, and
- **97% with auto, homeowners, life and health policies!**

While these figures are illustrative of the insurance business, the same principle is true of most other businesses. Banks, for instance, have studies that show the difference in customer retention with a customer that only has a checking account, versus another customer with multiple checking accounts, a savings account, an IRA, Safety Deposit box, their car financed through the bank, and a number of other services.

The idea is that by serving all the needs your prospects or customers have with the products and services you provide or have access to, you lock yourself in and the competition out.

And obviously, the longer you retain your customers, the more income you will earn from them, the more chances you will have to sell them additional products and services, and the more referrals you can get from them. It all adds up to increased profits for you.

Retention of your customers... the ones you've spent so much time, effort and money attracting and convincing to do business with you is critically important.

More than one study suggests that it costs six times more to get a prospect to buy from you than it does to get an existing customer to purchase from you again, and that it's sixteen times easier to sell an existing customer than it is a new prospect.

When you add it all up, for every 5% increase in customer retention, you'll generate a 30% to 45% increase in profitability over an 18 month period.

Depending on the nature of the products and services you sell, if your repurchase rate isn't in the high 90 percentile range, you have some work to do.

A lost customer is more than just a lost customer, and their attending profits. It's much more. In future chapters, we'll be discussing how to determine what the actual cost of a lost customer is, and what to do to prevent them from leaving.

But for now, just keep this important point in mind... if you're going to be successful in business, no matter what type of products or services you sell, you've got to have an intense focus on your customer. You've got to find out what they want and do everything you can to help them get it.

And if you want to make a fortune rather than just a living, you can't do it for only a few. You must do it for large numbers of people.

The success of your business will depend on how well you serve your customers... the people who buy from you!

Jon Riley. This chapter is all about creating **"Consistent Customers"**. Once you have loyal customers who know they can count on you, you may want to increase your prices. This is one way to give yourself a raise. Your customers won't mind paying more for great service. In Step 3 Growing your Business with my **Small Business Blueprint**, I explain how to increase your profits. You are in control of your business, it does not control you. If you do 250 jobs a year and raise your service charge by $20 that is an extra $5,000 to fund your **ROTH IRA** or to put more money into your company sponsored **S.E.P. IRA**. 25% of your income. **www.JonRileyIRA.com** for more info. It's time to:

GROW YOUR BUSINESS!

"Our deeds determine us as much as we determine our deeds."
George Eliot

The Four Primary Ways to Grow Your Business

Maximizing the Return on Your Efforts in the Four Key and Critical Areas

The number one thing... and one of the most important things for any business owner, manager, entrepreneur or professional to realize, is that there are four ways... four *principal* ways to grow a business – any business.

There are many things you can do to grow your business, but for purposes of our discussion here, we'll be focusing on four primary things.

The truth is that other than some administrative functions, some of which are not under your direct influence or control, nearly everything you do to build or grow your business can be classified under one of four different and distinct areas, or categories, and if you learn this one simple concept and how to apply it, believe me, your competition won't stand a chance.

And the reason?

Because your competition not only doesn't understand this concept, most of them have never even heard of it.

Now, here's the first one of the four ways to grow your business. Simply...

Get More Customers

That's it. Build your customer base. Get more prospects to buy from you and become your customers.

You know how it works. When more people buy from you, you take in more gross dollars, and as a result (depending on your margins and overhead), you make more bottom line profits.

As a spin-off benefit, the more people you add to your customer base the larger it becomes, and the larger it becomes the more people you have to go back to for additional sales and the referrals they're capable of giving you.

It's in this one single area where most business owners (including your competition, and probably, you, too, if you're honest), spend most of their time, effort and money.

If you've been in business for any length of time, you probably realize that getting new customers is not always the easiest, the most time-efficient, or most profitable thing you can do.

Most businesses only have one or two main methods of attracting new prospects to their businesses.

For example, you probably know that a large number of businesses are heavy in the use of telephone soliciting.

In fact, you, yourself, have probably gotten more than your fair share of calls, when you were just sitting down for dinner.

Chiropractors, car dealers, truck driving schools, and lawyers take a different approach. Many of them advertise heavily on television, especially during the afternoon hours to attract new customers. They've found that a large part of their intended audience… the people who are most inclined to use their services, watch television during those hours, and it's a cost-effective way to reach them.

Each business, industry, or profession has their own methods and timing to contact those who are most likely to be interested in their products and services. What works for some businesses, may or may not work for other businesses in the same or different industries or professions.

Think about your business and your company for a minute. Chances are, that you, like nearly every other business owner in your industry or profession also utilizes one, or perhaps two main methods of attracting new prospects.

Most likely, the method you use is the same method that nearly every other business uses. It's called the, *"That's how things are done in our industry or profession,"* method.

Typically, when a person first chooses to go into business they look around and see what everyone else is doing.

Then they layout their office, shop or place of business just like every other similar type of business they've seen.

They look at what everyone else is doing to market or promote their businesses, products and services, and adopt those same marketing plans and methods to market or promote their business.

This activity isn't isolated to just a few businesses – nearly every business in nearly every industry or profession is guilty.

But, wait a minute. Who set up that system in the first place? And who says it's right, or that it's the best system for you to use? The fact is, that there are an unlimited number of methods of attracting new customers to your business, and your imagination is the only limiting factor.

Some of the best, most productive and cost-effective methods you can use, can be adapted from what others are doing in totally unrelated businesses.

Now, this brings up a couple of questions. First, how observant are you? What are others who are in the same business that you're in doing? And, how effective are they?

Next, look around at what other businesses... unrelated businesses in other, unrelated fields, industries or professions are doing. Have you seen what's working for them? Is there one business that just stands out, by doing something different or unusual? Or, do they all pretty much use the same marketing methods?

Next question: How creative are you? Can you look at what some of the other businesses are doing, and adapt (with a few minor changes), their methods to your business?

In other words, if you were brand new, just starting in business, and had no idea of what anyone before you had done to attract new customers, what would you do? How would you go about getting new customers? Would you use the same methods you use now, or would you do something completely different?

A dentist I consult with specializes in working with children and their teeth. He loves children. And he recognizes that as they get older, they may need braces, they'll probably get married, and have a spouse and children that will all need dental care.

So, he set up his reception room with a special, "kid-height" counter, so when the children come in, they can talk directly to the receptionist, transact their business just as an adult would, and schedule their next appointment. He's even decorated his reception area with artwork and pictures that some of his young patients have created.

How do you think those young people feel? Well, you probably guessed it. They absolutely love it there. And they tell their friends about it, too. And their parents? They're *thrilled*.

Imagine, having your kids *want* to go to the dentist! And then be treated, not like a second-class citizen, but as an equal, transacting business (with the parent's help, of course), and having a hand in scheduling their future appointments.

What a learning and growing experience for them. And who do you think the parents use for their own dentist? That's right.

The spin-off business of catering to, and working with children, is their parents.

As the kids grow up and have families of their own, which dentist do you think they'll use… that they'll insist their spouse switches to, and that they'll bring their own children to?

The relationship this dentist is building with those young people… of friendship, of trust and of caring, will provide him all

the financial security he'll ever need, and allow him to do whatever he wants, and go wherever he pleases for the rest of his life.

So, what about you and your business? What are you doing? Specifically, what marketing methods are you using, *right now* to attract new customers, and to build lasting relationships with them so they'll do business with you for a lifetime?

And second, how many *different* marketing methods do you presently, and concurrently, have working for you? There's a real danger in having just one or two main methods of attracting new customers.

One of my consulting clients depended almost entirely on a telemarketing team to acquire leads for their salespeople to follow up with. When a well-funded competitor opened for business not far away, they hired nearly all that business' telemarketing staff, and nearly shut the business down. The business was nearly a total disaster.

When they called me in as a consultant, I could see that we had to do something quick, just to save the business. So, we got to work and hired and trained a whole new telemarketing crew, and got the business up and running again.

But then we looked at other marketing options and put together an effective direct-mail program, started a proactive referral-generating system, and worked out some joint ventures and host-beneficiary relationships with other, complementary, but non-competing businesses.

Now, if something happens to any one of their marketing methods, they have other strategies or other "pillars" in place that can keep the business from collapsing, and keep it running smoothly.

What about your business? How can you apply this?

Well, why not start by going back and revisiting the questions I asked earlier. Then see if there are some areas that you need to improve in.

Make sure you're not dependent on only one or two main methods of attracting new customers.

New customers are important to your business, there's no question. But, they're not just important, they're absolutely vital… not only to the growth of your business, but to the very survival of the business.

It's critical that you have multiple systems in place to ensure that your business continues running, *and growing*, uninterrupted, if anything unexpected happens.

Because of the limited amount of space in these pages, we can't talk about all the methods of getting new customers, but in the training materials and workshops we conduct, we go into great detail on effective ways to attract prospects by the bushel, and convert them into loyal, long-term customers.

As important as getting more new customers is, there are still three more methods you can use to grow your business. And each of these methods are more profitable, more effective, and give you greater potential for leverage than the first method.

Let's talk about number two...

Get Your Customers to Make Larger Average Purchases

In other words, increase the average transactional value of their purchases. Or more simply, get them to spend more money when they buy something from you.

This just happens to be the quickest and easiest way there is to increase your profits. One of the things that continually amazes me is the number of businesses that have *extensive* and *expensive* plans in place to acquire more customers.

Yet, very few have paid much attention to this highly profitable, and highly leverageable step of increasing the size of the order... getting more money from each of your customers every time they buy from you.

If you think for a minute about how easy this is and how profitable it can be, you'll see why it's such a powerful concept. And, you'll also see why nearly every fast-food restaurant has embraced, has mastered, and requires that every person who takes orders, understands, and is proficient in the use of the "up-sell" and "cross-selling" principles.

Think back about your own fast-food restaurant experience. You drive up to the speaker and place your order... a sandwich and a drink. And then what happens? A voice comes back over the speaker and asks if you'd like an apple pie, or fries with your order.

That's an example of cross-selling. Selling an additional product in addition to, or beyond the initial purchase.

Or, they might suggest that you "super-size" or "giant-size" your order. That's an example of an up-sell... increasing the size of the initial order.

In any case, if you take them up on their suggestion, what they've done is just increase their profits *substantially*, since they made an additional sale, but had no acquisition or marketing costs.

You see, they realize that a certain percentage of their customers will say, "Yes." And the only reason they say, "Yes," is because a suggestion was made to them. So they play the numbers game.

And the result? Well, by being aware of what their customers might want, but not ask for on their own, and then by asking questions or making suggestions, they bring in a substantial number of dollars. And other than the actual cost of the product, those dollars are pure profit.

Here's another technique fast food restaurants frequently use. It's called "bundling," or "packaging."

It's where they combine a sandwich, a drink and fries, then throw in a couple of "bonus" items, like maybe a cookie and a toy. They put it all together in one package, and give it a name like "Happy Meal."

They'll charge you less for that package than what each of those items purchased separately would have cost, but the total dollar amount you spend will be higher.

And, since there were no marketing costs involved, other than the cost of the items, themselves, its pure profit, and it goes straight to their bottom line.

Now, what does that have to do with you, and your business?

Well, you may not be in the fast food business, but the same principles can still apply. Just ask yourself this question: "What additional products or services do you have that would be natural complements to what your customers initially buy from you?"

Well, you know the answer to that and I won't go into all the details here. But for instance, if you have the type of business that offers more than one product to your customers you have a tremendous advantage to capitalize on the up-selling, cross-selling and bundling techniques.

Some types of businesses, such as insurance companies that may offer only one product or service can also benefit from these strategies by packaging certain policies that cover multiple family members, adding riders, or including other complementary services that go beyond the actual policies themselves.

Do these things seem like common sense to you? Well, they probably do. But as I mentioned before, it's surprising how few businesses make effective use these three simple principles.

Think about it. In reality, you have an obligation to your customers... the people who trust you to provide them good quality products and services, give them sound advice and who hand over their hard-earned money to you... to make sure they get the very best value, the best use and the most enjoyment from their original purchase.

And if you have additional items, either products or services, that can enhance their value, their use or their enjoyment, then your obligation is to do everything that's reasonable and ethical to see that they at least have the option of taking advantage of those items.

Again, it's playing the numbers game. Some will take advantage of your offer, and some won't. But at least you will have given them the opportunity, and you will have fulfilled your obligation to them.

You haven't made the decision for them. You've given them a choice, and you've let them decide.

If you come across as sincere, they'll not see you as being pushy, but they'll realize that you are really trying to do them a favor... to help them get more value, more use, and more benefit from their decision and their purchase.

And they'll come back to do business with you again, and again, and will refer others to you, as well.

Up-selling, cross-selling and bundling... these are only three of more than a dozen immediate, profit-producing methods you can use to skyrocket your business to the next level.

If you do nothing more than find a way to incorporate these three techniques in your business (which you should be able to do within the next twenty-four hours), you'll blast your profits completely through the roof.

Think about it... increasing your sales... increasing your *profits*... without increasing your expenses. It's an exciting concept, and it can add an *immediate* twenty, thirty, even forty percent or more, *in pure profits* to your bottom line!

Now, let's move on to the third way to grow your business…

Get Your Customers to Buy From You More Often

In other words, increase the frequency of their purchases. Get them to come back, Give them reasons to *want* to come back and to continue doing business with you. The longer your customers go between purchases from you, the more chance they have of buying from your competition.

It's like, "Out of sight, out of mind." You need to constantly stay in front of your customers with educational information, and notices of changes in the law or updates regarding the products or services they've purchased from you that can affect them. And you need to tell them about new products, new lines, special incentives and other offers that might benefit them.

The idea, is two-fold: One, to "lock" your customers in, so they can't afford to do business with anyone else, and secondly, to make it so attractive to do business with you, that they wouldn't even consider going anywhere else.

What you really want to do, is lead your customers to the inescapable and undeniable conclusion, that they would have to be completely out of their minds to even consider doing business with anyone else but you, regardless of the selection of products or services you provide, the prices you charge, your location, or the relationship they may have with the business they're currently doing business with.

Let me give you some real life examples of how this works: One of the clients I consult with owns a restaurant. And for his business customers who like to take their clients to lunch, he offers a certain number of lunches for a pre-paid, discounted price.

By doing this, he "locks in" his customer, gets his money up-front, and makes it convenient for everyone. The customer simply signs the check, which includes the tip. No money changes hands during or after the lunch, and new customers are constantly being introduced to his restaurant. As a result, many of those new customers take advantage of the same arrangement for their clients.

Here's another example. The car wash where I take my cars offers a special pre-paid, discounted card, that's good for a certain number of car washes. It's a great deal for me because I save money, and I can take my car to be washed, even if my teenagers have gotten into my wallet and taken the last couple of dollars I had.

And when my card is filled, I've got a free wax job coming. It's a good deal for the car wash too, because they've gotten their money up front, and have locked me out of the competition.

Here's one more. The store my wife buys shoes from offers "points" program. Every so often, she receives a notice in the mail informing her of how many points she's accumulated. Now, she may not have been to that store for quite a while, but when she gets that notice and sees the credit she has coming, she nearly always makes it back to that store within just a couple of days. And she hardly ever leaves empty handed.

Airlines offer upgrades and mileage bonuses for those who fly with them on a regular basis. And countless other businesses offer similar programs as well.

Now, let's apply this concept to you and your business. What can you think of that you could do, that will endear your customers to you? To lock them in, and get them coming back more often, and even refer others to do business with you?

Do you have an educational newsletter or special informative reports that you periodically send them that keeps them updated?

Do you send postcards, or do you have a website that keeps them informed of new items and promotions?

Do you hold special "Customer Appreciation Sales" or events?

How about a frequent buyer club for your more loyal customers?

What about a Referral Reward system that recognizes or compensates your customers for referring their friends?

You've got to let your customers know that you value them, that you appreciate them, that you want them to come back, and you want to make doing business with you fun, risk-free, rewarding, and easy.

Well, I'm sure you can see that the ideas are unlimited. And while the restaurant, car wash and shoe store examples may not apply directly to your business, I've included them to serve as a stimulus so you can begin thinking of what you might consider applying in your business that can help you develop trust and loyalty with your customers.

In our coaching programs we go into great detail, and discuss more than two-dozen very specific strategies that create an almost magnetic effect, that keeps your customers returning time and time again.

We lead you by the hand and help you develop personalized and effective strategies that keep them saying, "I'll be back"… strategies that keep them "insulated" from, and locked out of your competition.

Now let's talk about the fourth method you can use to grow your business. And that is, to…

Extend Your Customers' "Average Buying Lifetime"

We call that, "Customer Retention."

Here's what I mean: How long, on average, do the people who buy from you, your customers, remain your customers?

In other words, how long do they continue doing business with you before they move on? Are they one-time buyers? Do they stay with you for a year, five years or ten years? Have you ever stopped to figure it out? This is an important step, and one that we'll be discussing in more detail in later pages.

Next, what are you doing in your business *right now*, to make sure your customers *continue* doing business with you? If you don't have a strategic plan, a *working system* in place, you are going to lose a certain percent of your current customers to the competition.

There's no question about it. Your competition… *right now*… *right this very minute*, is making plans and taking steps to take your customers away from you.

The question for you, is not, "What are you going to do about it?"

The *real* question is, "What are you *currently* doing about it?"

"What are you doing about it *right now*?"

What plans… what *systems* do you have in place to keep your customers from defecting to the competition?

Let's talk about your customers for a minute. Are they *thrilled* enough with the products you offer and the services they receive from you to continue doing business with you year after year?

What if you answered "yes" to that question?

My next questions would be, "Are you sure?"

"How do you know?"

"Where did you get your information?"

"How reliable is it?"

"Can you explain in detail, the *system* you have in place for finding out?"

Notice that I said, "Are they *thrilled* enough?" Not "are they *satisfied* enough?" You see, there's a big difference between being *thrilled* and being *satisfied*.

One year, more than 200 million Americans stopped doing business with companies that they were "satisfied" with. And sixty percent of so-called "satisfied" customers switch companies or brands on a regular basis.

As a business owner, you can't afford not to thrill your customers, nor to build trust in you and your business. The cost is too high, and unfortunately, most business owners simply don't understand it. Let's take a look at what the potential cost could be to you if you fail to do these things:

Let's say that you make $200 in sales per year from your average customer.

And let's say that for any number of reasons, 100 customers stop doing business with you each year. They may die or move away. They may no longer have need for your products or services, they may switch companies, have a relative in the business, or possibly have a bad experience with someone in your company.

Or, they may just simply disagree with some policy or procedure you might have. It could be a falling out with a staff member or employee, a personality conflict, miscommunication, a problem they had with one of your products, or perhaps a feeling of neglect from you or someone in your business. It really doesn't matter what the reason, they just stop doing business with you.

Well, those 100 customers no longer paying you $200 this year just cost you $20,000. But, that's not all. What if those 100 customers tell 5 others about their experience with you?

That's an additional 500 potential customers who won't be doing business with you this year (or maybe ever, for that matter).

And if each of them spent an average of $200, that's $100,000 you won't be receiving from them, *PLUS* the $20,000 you lost on your existing customers who left.

That brings the total in lost income to *$120,000 in just one year!*

It's not unusual for some businesses to bring in a hundred (or more) new customers each month. That's twelve hundred-plus, customers a year. And they end up only netting a 150 or 200 increase at year-end (sometimes not even that).

Well, what happened to the other more than 1,000 customers? Where did they go? Surely, they all didn't die, or move away.

But, you know, most business owners don't concern themselves with what, or whom they've lost. They just focus on their net gain. They figure that if they finish the year with more customers or more sales than they started with, they're ahead.

Now, let's suppose that you gave those 100 lost customers reasons,… good, compelling, life or business enhancing reasons, to continue doing business with you this year.

And let's suppose each of them told those same five people about their now-positive experience with you.

Well, there's $20,000 you wouldn't have lost in the first place, and another $100,000 you may possibly pick up from their referrals or by their word of mouth.

The point is, customers are important – *all* customers. In fact, they're critical. There's no question about it. You and I both know that. A business couldn't remain in business unless it has someone to buy its products and services.

Those "someone's" are people. Real people. People like you and like me. If you sell your products to the business community, remember, businesses don't buy from businesses.

People in business buy from other people in business. It's people that you market to. Not businesses.

Here's an interesting point: Most business owners know exactly how much they have tied up in furniture, fixtures and equipment. They can tell you, nearly to the penny, how much each item costs, how old it is, how much it's depreciated and what the remaining life expectancy is.

That's important information for any business to have. There's no question about it. But what's amazing is that very few business owners have any idea of what the value of their most important asset is... their customers.

Think about how this whole concept relates to your business, for a minute. What is it that you can do, *specifically*, to extend your customer's buying lifetime with you? Why not take a few minutes and answer these questions?

First of all, who are your customers ... those who are buying from you now?

Who are their family members?

Do you know the names and ages of their spouse or children?

Do you know where they work?

What about their spouse or children?

What are their hobbies or interests?

Do you know why they purchased a certain type of product or service?

Do you know who their friends, neighbors or relatives are?

What about your staff or employees? Do you know how they treat or feel about your customers?

Do they, or do you, for that matter, have *favorite* customers? What makes them a "favorite?" Is it how much they spend? How often they come in? Their personality? And how do you treat those customers? Any different than the others?

Do you have regular staff meetings and talk about how to think like a customer?

What you would want if you were a prospect considering doing business with you for the first time? Or maybe an existing customer considering giving repeat business to your establishment or organization?

Or, perhaps considering referring a friend, a family member or an acquaintance?

Do you have a training system in place to teach your staff how to handle or deal with difficult customers? Short-tempered customers? Analytical customers?

Do you have a plan for moving people up the "Loyalty Ladder?" From Suspect to Prospect to Shopper. Then on to Customer, Client, and Advocate. And, finally to convert them into Raving Fans?

When a customer stops doing business with you, do you know why? Do you have a *system* in place to find out?

What would you have to do differently to get your customers to buy from you for, say, 5 ½ years, instead of just 5 years?

Believe me, if you will actually take the time to go through these questions and formulate answers for them, and then incorporate that information into your business practices, you can work wonders towards extending the buying lifetime of your customers. And as a result, you'll add *significant* profits to your bottom line.

We've covered a lot of ground and a lot of ideas, so far. So, let's pause for a minute, and recap what we've discussed up to this point. There are four primary ways to grow a business.

First, **get more customers**. And as I mentioned, this is a vital step. But it's also the most difficult and the most costly.

Second, **get your customers to spend more money with you**… increase the average transactional value of each sale. And remember that this is the fastest and the easiest way to add immediate profits to your bottom line.

Third, **get your customers coming back to buy from you more often**.

And, fourth, **extend your customers' buying lifetime**. Find ways to retain them, keep them as customers and keep them coming back as long as you possibly can. It's really pretty simple. Nearly everything you do to build and grow your business can be slotted under one of these four categories. As I mentioned earlier, there are more than two-dozen ways to apply these concepts and build your business, but for now, if you'll work on these four primary methods, you'll absolutely run circles around your competitors.

As you take a good, close-up look at these four areas, you'll see that what it really boils down to, is effectively marketing your business to your customers and potential customers.

In other words, the success of your business enterprise depends, largely, on how effective your marketing system is.

And that means that if you want your business to excel... to really excel... if you want to virtually eliminate your competition, and become the dominating force in your marketplace, then you've got to begin thinking of yourself as being in the *marketing* business, not in the product or service selling business.

In effect, you need to consider yourself as the head of a marketing organization that sells the products and services that your business offers.

Once you begin operating effectively at that point, you'll find that your job becomes much easier and much more enjoyable, and your prospects and customers will begin seeking you out and referring others to you, rather than you chasing after them. The net result will be that your marketing costs will plummet, and your profits will skyrocket!

Jon Riley. Blah, blah, blah is mostly what I heard. We get it, this number times this number will get you this number. If you're still awake, let's break it down. It is not hard to **build a following of loyal customers** if you have a small one or two-person business and you follow my process. But if you want to grow your business and hire people, you will have to attract more customers to support your new employees. This is an area I have avoided. When you hire one person on the payroll, you have to get workman's compensation insurance. This could be a blessing or the worst thing ever. Most of my friends who have big companies do not seem happy. **Excessive drinking and hair loss could be a result of hiring employees.** Use sub-contractors and 1099 them to avoid it. Being responsible for Holiday bonuses and other people's family is a huge responsibility. It can also come with great rewards as well. A 2-person team is as far as I can take you. In my experience a 2-person team can produce up to $250,000 a year in a **Service Type Business.** If you want to make more money, then build a team and keep going. The sky is the limit. Let's talk about the value of a:

CUSTOMER.

"Only a life lived for others is a life worthwhile."
Albert Einstein

How Much Are Your Customers Really Worth?

Determining the Lifetime Profit Value of Your Customers

There's not much debate about this fact: Your existing customers or clients are your most valuable assets. The question is, how much are they worth?

How much money… how much *profit* will you realize from each of your customers, over their "buying lifetime" with you?

This is such an important concept, and I can't say it strongly enough, that just knowing and understanding this one thing can have a bigger impact on your business than just about anything else you can do.

Once you understand it, a whole new set of factors will come into play, and can absolutely revolutionize the way you look at your business, the way you *do* business, and the profits you'll generate as a result. Let me give you an example to explain what I mean.

Let's say that your average sale is $50. And let's say that your average customer buys from you 4 times per year.

So from those four transactions, you realize $200 in income. And let's say that this customer does business with you on average, for 10 years. Over that 10-year period (or their "lifetime" of doing business with you), that average customer has been worth $2,000 in income to you.

Now, let's expand this example to a theoretical base of 1,000 customers and see what it means. Those 1,000 customers at $200 a year nets you an annual income of $200,000.

Let's assume that with the proper programs in place that you're able to increase each of the 4 ways to grow your business that we discussed earlier, by only 10 percent. Here's what happens:

First, the number of customers you have, increases from 1,000 to 1,100.

Next, the average transaction amount per sale increases from $50 to $55.

Third, the average number of purchases per customer increases from 4 times 4.4 times.

So, the annual income from your customer base will increase from $200,000 ($50 x 4 transactions x 1,000 customers) to $266,200 ($55 x 4.4 x 1,100 customers). That's an increase of $66,200 a year!

That's a huge increase!

But if you think that's exciting, wait till you see what happens if you were to extend your customer's buying lifetime by just 10 percent.

Let's say that your customers stay with you for 10 years, on average. Your lifetime value from those customers over that period of time would normally be $2,000,000. But, if you can extend that 10 years by just 10 percent to 11 years, your total dollar value from these customers will increase from $2,000,000 to $2,928,200 ($266,200 x 11 years)!

An increase of $928,200... nearly a million dollars! That's a *major* increase!

But that's not all. Let's say that you put an effective referral generating system in place, and that just 10 percent of your 1,000 customers sends you a referral with a buying profile the same as your average customer.

That's an additional 100 customers who will bring you income of another $266,200 over the 11 years ($55 x 4.4 renewals x 100 customers x 11 years).

Total it all up, and you just made an additional $1,194,400! That's an average of $1,085,818 per year over the 11 years! Sound impossible? Well, it's not. And it's not all that difficult, either. It can be done by simply increasing each of the four areas by only 10 percent!

Now, how hard would that be to do in your business? Could you realistically, and with some help, increase each of the four areas we discussed, by ten percent? What about twenty percent?

Some of the businesses I consult with, after realizing the power of this key concept, and the others that we've discussed, have increased their businesses by as much as a hundred percent, or more in less than a year.

Maybe the numbers and figures I've discussed are realistic for you and your business, and maybe they're not. And maybe you can't increase each of the areas by the same percentage. That's okay. That doesn't matter.

The point is you probably have room for improvement in one, or more of the four areas. And if you want your business to be a viable force in the marketplace, and to give you the lifestyle, the satisfaction and the income you want, you're going to have to take some proactive steps.

Knowing the Value of Your Customers Influences the Way You Treat Them

As I mentioned before, just knowing how much your customers are worth to you can be invaluable, and can help you in several ways.

First of all, we know that people don't do business with the same company or business forever. They stop doing business or change whom they do business with for a variety of reasons, and we've already discussed some of those.

But, if you just know, for instance, that your typical customer stays with you for say, ten years, on average, that they're not just a one or two-time sale, you may begin to treat them differently.

You may treat them with more respect, more kindness, and more courtesy. You may give them some form of special treatment. And you may even invite them to special, invitation-only, preferred customer seminars or events.

In other words, once you begin to see your customers in a different light, you may begin to do things differently in order to get them to stay longer as customers.

Next, if you know what the Lifetime Profit Value of your customers is, you'll probably discover that you can spend far more to acquire a new customer than you originally thought.

In other words, if your average customer is worth $2,000 in income to you, you can, theoretically, afford to spend up to $2,000 to bring in a new customer and still break even.

In theory, you could spend that $2,000 and still make a profit on the other "back end" products that you might be able to sell them.

And, if you put an effective referral-generating program in place, you can spend that same $2,000, and make your profits on the referrals they generate.

You and I both know that it's unrealistic to think that you can really afford to spend the full amount of your lifetime income (in this case, $2,000), to get each new customer. And I'm certainly not suggesting that.

In reality, you *can't* spend the entire $2,000. You've got to be concerned about things like overhead, cash-flow and reserves. You can't spend money you don't have.

And, you have to make sure that the customers you attract, at least match the profile of your average customers, or perhaps are even a little better than average.

There are a number of other things that you need to be aware of, as well, such as, "Cost of Acquisition," "Cost of Retention," understanding your margins, and calculating the Marginal Net Worth of your customers.

Unfortunately, we don't have time to cover them in sufficient detail, here.

Knowing the Value of Your Customers Influences How Much You Can Spend to Get a New One, or Keep an Existing One

What it really comes down to are two questions: How much can you *afford* to spend, and how much are you *willing* to spend to attract new business?

You may find that you can, and are willing to spend five or six times what your competitors spend. And if they're not willing to keep up with you, your business may just explode and leave them in the dust.

Just knowing what your *margins* are, and that you could, if you had to, spend up to that $2,000 amount and still break even, gives you a *tremendous* edge over your competition.

Here's a real-life example: My wife and I have a favorite restaurant we like to go to about twice a month. And our meals typically come to about $30. So, $30 times 24 meals add up to $720 in gross sales for the year.

Let's suppose that we continue to patronize that restaurant for, say, 10 years. That's our buying lifetime with that particular restaurant. That gives the restaurant a total of $7,200 in sales.

If over that 10-year period, we refer 10 people, 5 of whom become regular customers (and that's not very many in 10 years), who have spending patterns similar to ours, they'll spend an additional $36,000. (That's 5 people, times $7,200 a year.)

Add that to the $7,200 that we spent, and we've been responsible for generating $43,200 for that restaurant. Even after deducting expenses for overhead, salaries and food costs, the restaurant still realizes a pretty substantial number of profit dollars from the efforts of just one couple.

Restaurant Example	
A. Amount of average sale	$ 30
B. No. of sales/year/customer (2 x per month)	24
C. Gross income per year per customer (A x B)	$ 720
D. No. of years customer patronizes restaurant	10
E. Gross income over buying lifetime (C x D)	$ 7,200
F. No. of referrals from customer over buying	10
G. % of referrals who become a customer	50 %
H. Referrals who become customers (G x F)	5
I. Gross income from referrals (E x H)	$ 36,000
J. Total value of a loyal customer (E + I)	**$ 43,200**

Now, here's a question: Could that restaurant afford to give away a free meal to attract a new customer? Keep in mind that two of us are spending $30, so one meal costs $15, and out of that, about a third of it (or, maybe $5) is profit.

So, the meal really only costs the restaurant $10 for the two meals, and only part of that $10 goes to cover the cost of the food.

The rest of the expense is in overhead, which would have to be paid whether or not a meal was served.

Well, of course the answer is yes, they *can* afford to give away a free meal. Not only that, but they can afford to do a number of other things to not only attract new customers, but more important, make their existing customers feel more appreciated and more special. And you know, when someone feels noticed and important, appreciated and special, it's just natural that they'll want to return.

Let's imagine, for a minute, that you are a long-time, faithful customer of a certain restaurant. And you brought your family, your clients or your business associates with you to eat there on a regular basis.

How would *you* feel, if sometime, the manager of the restaurant were to offer you and your party a free dessert as a special appreciation gift for your loyalty and for the extra business you brought them? Do you think that little display of appreciation would cause you to want to return again? I think it's pretty safe to say that it probably would.

And what about the people who were with you? How do you think they would feel? Do you think they would want to go back to that restaurant? Sure, they would. What do you think the restaurant's hard costs of those desserts would be? Do you think the restaurant would lose any money on that gesture?

Well, it's not likely. You see, once you know how much profit your customers are worth to you, long term, then, and only then, can you determine how much you can afford to give away, or to spend, to get new customers, or to keep your existing customers coming back. And you can begin to experiment with different offers to see which ones work best.

Now, here's another thought. Let's say that the owner of that restaurant runs an ad, or does a mailing to attract new customers.

And let's say he spends $1,000 for the ad or the mailing, and two couples come in for dinner, and each spends $30.

Well, he's taken in a total of $60. But the ad costs were $1,000. So what does he do? What would his competition do?

Does he consider the ad or mail campaign a loser... a total bust... and stop running it? That's what most business people do.

But what about you? What would you do? Well, if you understand the concept of Lifetime Profit Value and Marginal Net Worth, you'll probably think differently.

When you consider the Lifetime Value of those customers and realize that with the proper care and attention those customers could be responsible for $43,200 each, or $86,400 for the two of them, it changes the picture.

Of course, those numbers are gross revenue figures, and you have to deduct for expenses. And it's over a 10-year period. But, still, that represents a significant amount of money. And all from a $1,000 ad. An ad that most business owners would have given up on.

Now, I'm not saying that you have to settle for, and be happy with low response rates for your ads. Certainly, you don't. You should always try to improve your ads, your letters, your offers... and give good, compelling reasons and benefits for someone to do business with you.

That's an entire subject, itself, and one we don't have time to discuss in great detail here. But one we take very seriously, and spend considerable time on in our workshops and coaching programs.

Let's go back and think about our restaurant example for a minute. Did this idea of stopping an ad just because it didn't break even, or produce a profit for you sound unusual? Different? Strange? Well, maybe to some people, in some businesses.

But, supermarkets and department stores use their own adaptation of this technique all the time. You've probably heard it referred to as a "loss leader."

What they do is advertise a few products at, or below cost to bring new customers in to their store, knowing that the customer will usually buy more products once they're in the store.

And also knowing, that unless they get someone to visit their store in the first place, they could never stand a chance of making additional or repeat sales, or getting referrals from them. And additional and repeat sales to existing customers are generally easier to make, and usually always bring higher profit margins.

Just remember this important point:

The first sale means nothing... unless you're planning on going out of business next week.
You've got to consider the Lifetime Profit Value...what your customer is worth to you,
if you really want to be successful.

Now, what about you, in your business? How can you apply this concept of Lifetime Profit Value?

Well, the first thing you can do is determine what the amount of your average income per sale is. The Lifetime Profit Value Calculator below is provided for you to use in calculating the Lifetime Profit Value of your own customers. Fill out with your current figures to get an idea of how much your customers are worth to you.

The LPV of Your Customers (Actual)	
A. Amount of average sale	$
B. No. of sales/year/customer (2 x per month)	
C. Gross income per year per customer (A x B)	$
D. No. of years customer patronizes restaurant	
E. Gross income over buying lifetime (C x D)	$
F. No. of referrals from customer over buying	
G. % of referrals who become a customer	%
H. Referrals who become customers (G x F)	
I. Gross income from referrals (E x H)	$
J. Total value of a loyal customer (E + I)	$

The calculator below is provided so you can calculate what kind of a difference it will make to your business if you increased each of the areas by 10 percent.

Keep in mind as you do these calculations, that this is a very simplified calculation. In our consulting sessions we get very detailed and take into consideration many more areas. So the results you'll see in actuality will be dramatically increased. But for a simple and easy to demonstrate way to determine your customers' value to you, these basic calculators will do quite nicely.

The LPV of Your Customers (+10%)	
A. Amount of average sale	$
B. No. of sales/year/customer (2 x per month)	
C. Gross income per year per customer (A x B)	$
D. No. of years customer patronizes restaurant	
E. Gross income over buying lifetime (C x D)	$
F. No. of referrals from customer over buying	
G. % of referrals who become a customer	%
H. Referrals who become customers (G x F)	
I. Gross income from referrals (E x H)	$
J. Total value of a loyal customer (E + I)	$

Jon Riley. Again so much math. Why? We get it numbers in and numbers out. You now get the value of a customer and how to calculate if you want. Bottom line is get off your ass and **Select** your Business, then **Serve** that business and then you will **Succeed** in that business. It's 3 simple steps. SELECT-SERVE-SUCCEED. You must Serve2Succeed. That is why I created the **S2S Small Business Academy**. It's 90 days of personal one on one coaching via recorded telephone or online video conference call. Followed up with e-mail, text and secret Facebook group support. It ends with **Live training in Los Angeles** where you will be awarded your Serve2Succeed certification. We will also take Green Screen pictures for your marketing. Then choose the best ones and have the green screen removed. I will send you the .png files and you can use them on your website, cards & flyers. One Year Members can also attend the event. I hope **"Consistent Customers"** opened up your eyes and put you in the **MINDSET** for business. Find someone who is doing exactly what you want to be doing and ask them to Mentor you. That is exactly what I am doing. Mentoring Small Business Entrepreneurs to:

"Live Life by Design and not by Default"

"When inspiration does not come to me, I go half way to meet it."
Sigmund Freud

Epilogue

Where Do You Go from Here?

Congratulations for making it this far. You have now been exposed to some of the most powerful and effective techniques, concepts and ideas available for succeeding in business.

But no matter how good these ideas are, just being exposed to them is not enough. You must also do something with them. In order for you to get the most value out of this material, you might want to consider developing a step-by-step action plan. An effective and results producing plan should consist of 5 areas:

1. EVALUATION

Ideas are nothing more than ideas until they are put into action. Once acted on, they have the potential to literally turn around a struggling business, or help an already successful business become even more dynamic and successful.

But before a person runs out and implements a new-found idea, they should first take the time to evaluate their operation to determine just what areas are most lacking and could use the most attention.

You have the potential of making the most improvement in your own business, if you will take the time to identify and work on the area of greatest need, first.

2. RESEARCH

Once you've identified your greatest needs and placed them in priority order, you can begin to search out available solutions. Be on an opportunity lookout. The material in this manual is just the beginning of the many places you can find good, usable, and practical ideas.

Don't turn any ideas away just because you think they might not pertain to your business or the way you operate. Capture them and then apply step number three.

3. PERSONALIZATION

As you encounter new ideas, keep an open mind. Study them. Analyze them. And think them through. Ask yourself if an application can be

made to your specific situation by simply changing or modifying part of the concept or idea.

If a certain illustration uses a certain type of product or service for the example, but you don't sell that product or service, a simple adjustment might be all that's needed.

The material in the book is designed to illustrate concepts, and only uses certain types of products as examples to make various points.

4. IMPLEMENTATION

Just as a membership in a health club won't do its owner any good unless he or she goes to the club and participates in the exercise program, so too, with the information in this book.

It's of no practical use unless it is implemented. It's easy to come up with good ideas and develop plans, but where most people get bogged down is when it comes to putting them into action. It's not always easy, but if you're going to truly be successful, you must do whatever it takes to act on your plans.

5. REVIEW

After you've worked with your new ideas for a period of time, stop and evaluate how things are working. You may need to make some adjustments so you can continue to see improvement.

Sometimes, an idea you thought was great doesn't work out at all. That's okay, don't continue using it. Just scrap it and move on to your next business adventure.

On the other hand, if you find an idea that works well, see if you can refine it, or "plus" it to make it even more effective.

That's all there is to it. Sounds simple enough to say, but in reality, there's a lot to do. The plain and truthful facts are, that most people simply won't take the time and effort to do the things we've just discussed. That's unfortunate on one hand, because they could be even more successful than they are now.

On the other hand, their failure to take action is good for you. Because if it's you that does these things and not them, it will be you who realizes the success. Now you have the tools.

GO FOR IT!

You now have a good *MINDSET* and understanding about customer relationships. If you or someone you know would like more information on "how to" *Start a Small Business*, you can find it on my website. Pass this book forward. *Hugs*, ... Jon

SCAN ME NOW!
www.YourBusinessWithin.com

CONSISTENT CUSTOMERS

"There is no traffic on that extra mile"

1. Select
2. Serve
3. Succeed

Jon Riley

www.ingramcontent.com/pod-product-compliance
Lightning Source LLC
Chambersburg PA
CBHW060403190526
45169CB00002B/729